Collins
Big Cat
Progress
Handbook

Written by Gillian Howell

Series Editor: Cliff Moon

Collins

Published by Collins
An imprint of HarperCollins*Publishers*
77–85 Fulham Palace Road
Hammersmith
London
W6 8JB

ISBN 978-0-00-747705-0

10 9 8 7 6 5 4 3 2 1

British Library Cataloguing in Publication Data
A catalogue record for this publication is available from the British Library.

Author: Gillian Howell
Series Editor: Cliff Moon
Designer: Neil Adams
Models: Malaysia John-Baptiste, Sabiom Leksian, Kevin Wambui, Lailei Winks
Illustrators: Bridget Dowty and Maggie Brand

APP authors: Clare Dowdall and Arthur Shenton
APP designer: Planman Technologies

Acknowledgements
Collins would like to thank Melcombe Primary School for their help with this book.

p5: Sarah Thomas/HarperCollins*Publishers*; p12: Sarah Thomas/HarperCollins*Publishers*; p13: Sarah Thomas/HarperCollins*Publishers*; p15: Monkey Business Images/Shutterstock; p30: FogStock/Alamy; p32: CliffParnell/iStockphoto; p33: Kali9/iStockphoto; p34, top: Image Source/Getty; p34, bottom: monkeybusinessimages/iStockphoto; p43: Darrin Henry/Shutterstock; p44: MBI/Alamy; p47: Juice Images/Alamy; p96: Juice Images/Alamy; p102: Seab De Burca/Corbis

Printed and bound by Martins the Printers, Berwick upon Tweed

Visit **www.collinsbigcat.com**
for more details on the whole series

Browse the complete Collins Education
catalogue at **www.collinseducation.com**

Contents

1   **Welcome to Collins Big Cat Progress**   4

2   **Identifying struggling readers**   30

3   **Collins Big Cat Progress in practice**   34

4   **Using APP to assess with confidence**   44

    Matching Charts   48

    Assessment Examples   60

    Running Records   84

5   **Integrating Collins Big Cat Progress with whole-class work**   96

6   **Collins Big Cat Progress and reading at home**   102

    Activity sheets   104

1 Welcome to Collins Big Cat Progress

Collins Big Cat is a reading series with a difference. The difference lies chiefly in the quality and variety of stories and factual books, written and illustrated by carefully selected authors and illustrators/photographers who know what children love – books which are indistinguishable from those found in bookshops and libraries and with themes of universal interest for children aged four to eleven. The books are levelled into a readability sequence to support teachers working on the book-match principle.

It is worth reminding ourselves, at the outset, of the general principles which underpin the Collins Big Cat core readers because these principles apply equally to Progress books, which cater for struggling and/or reluctant readers. These general principles can be summarised as follows:

- learning to read is an holistic process
- positive attitudes to reading are vital
- book levelling supports development
- natural language makes reading more accessible
- visual literacy supports comprehension
- children need to be exposed to a range of fiction and non-fiction genres
- children need to understand and respond creatively to what they have read.

To these we can add the following principles that are more specific to Progress books:

- every child has a right of access to the whole curriculum
- struggling readers deserve the best
- boys, in particular, need books that capture their interests
- all children have the right to 'find themselves in a book'
- parents/carers have a role to play too.

We'll briefly summarise each of these principles in turn …

Learning to read is an holistic process

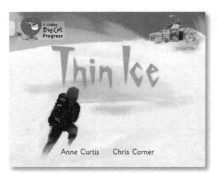

Learning to read is much the same as learning to do anything else. In order to read fluently you have to co-ordinate a range of strategies at the same time, e.g. attending to semantic, syntactic and grapho-phonemic cues. Think of learning to swim, walk or talk – what helps or hinders learning these skills?

Struggling readers often run the risk of perceiving reading as a fragmented activity due to an emphasis on learning a set of sub-skills. They need to know that in order to read fluently they should search for meaning in a variety of ways, simultaneously using all available cues. This often leads to approximations rather than strict word-for-word accuracy, as when a child substitutes "house" for "home" which is similar in meaning, part-of-speech, word shape and initial letter sound – what has been termed "reading as a psycholinguistic guessing game". With Progress books, which are rich in content and meaning, this process is easily facilitated.

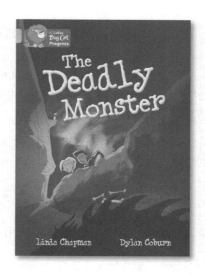

Positive attitudes to reading are vital

Children who are reluctant to read have often been put off reading because they haven't encountered sufficiently interesting or motivating reading material to read for themselves or to have read to them. Children who struggle with reading frequently fail to experience the intrinsic rewards for the efforts they make. Why? Because there are too few rewards on offer! Collins Big Cat provides a unique resource which rewards readers at every turn because all the books have intrinsic literary merit with a quality in authorship and illustration equal to the best children's books on the market, and helps them see themselves as real readers. As Margaret Meek commented, "What the beginning reader reads makes all the difference to his/her view of reading." The books we put in front of struggling or reluctant readers need to present a different reading experience from the one they might expect; they need to engage and enchant, inform and interest, and therefore redefine the child's perception of reading.

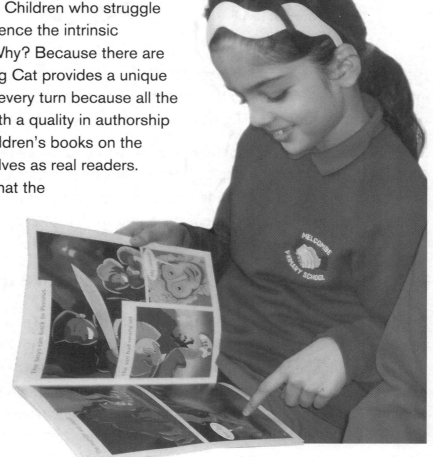

Book levelling supports development

All children need books they *can*, rather than *can't* read. Matching the reading competence of the child to the readability of the text facilitates the reading process right from the start. Collins Big Cat books are levelled in line with the Institute of Education's Book Bands for Guided Reading for Bands 1A–11, with the additional KS2 Bands 12–18 and Band 0 (wordless picture books). This provides useful guidance for both children and teachers. Children can steer themselves towards books that are within their competence and teachers can be confident that their children are being sufficiently challenged in their reading – and structure their progression coherently.

There are two book band indicators on each Progress back cover: the upper denotes the readability of the text, the lower denotes the book's interest level.

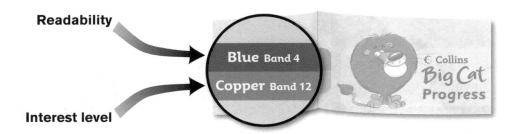

Be flexible – book matching is meant to be a guideline only. When children are particularly interested in a story or topic their match point can be anything up to four bands higher than usual. Similarly, for struggling readers, allow for a corresponding drop in bands.

Remember the independent (99% accuracy), instructional (95% accuracy) and frustration (90% accuracy) levels? Independent level is useful for home reading as children can read unaided; instructional level is ideal for supported reading whereas frustration level is best avoided at all costs – comprehension is below 50% at this level.

Natural language makes reading more accessible

By trialling every Collins Big Cat book in schools we have tried to ensure that the texts are as close as possible to what most children would expect from the context. This supports their developing confidence and desire to "have a go" – especially important for those who find reading difficult. There is also the issue of how much exposure children have had to written language conventions. It has been estimated that some children will have had up to 8000 stories read aloud to them before they begin school; other children may have had none. Therefore the fortunate ones will have internalised the patterns of written language and know what to expect.

This is why, for example, Collins Big Cat books up to and including Band 5 (Green) make more use of the pre-cued speech form rather than the usual written language post-cued convention.

pre-cued speech

And we have taken further steps towards helping novice readers to read naturally in the early readability bands, for example:

- Conjunctions like *and* and *but* are placed at the ends of lines to signal that there is more to follow

- Articles and their nouns are not split by line breaks

- First words of sentences appear only at the beginnings of lines

- Extensive use of ellipses … to encourage anticipation and prediction.

ellipses

Reading words that immediately sound familiar should not only make the texts more accessible, but the environment more comfortable and in turn the reader more relaxed – especially important for those to whom it comes less naturally.

Visual literacy supports comprehension

Reading the illustrations and filling the gaps – both text and illustrations contribute to the overall meaning. This is particularly true of the graphic fiction and non-fiction to be found in the Progress strand. They are so much more than text alone – some children will be able to explore plots, characters and themes in more depth through "reading" the artwork whereas others can access the text on a simpler, more literal level. Take *In the Game* as an example: the two protagonists are so involved in their interactive computer game they fail to notice the alien invasion taking place behind their backs, yet the reader is let in on the secret. After the mayhem is over and the flying saucers depart, the pair set off for home saying, "Not much is happening here." It's the pantomime ghost syndrome, full of irony and humour.

Children need to be exposed to a range of fiction and non-fiction genres

Collins Big Cat provides a full range of reading experiences from traditional tales, fantasy, humorous and historical stories to non-fiction explanations and instructions, recounts and biographies. This gives children a broad and exciting reading experience throughout the primary years.

Here is the range of genres represented in the Progress books:

- Graphic novel
- Humour
- Fantasy
- Mystery
- Adventure
- Non-chronological report
- Information book
- Recount
- Report
- Science fiction
- Stories from other cultures

An information book

A story from another culture

A mystery story

A graphic novel

A non-chronological report

A science fiction story

An information book

Children need to understand and respond creatively to what they have read

Every Collins Big Cat book concludes with a double-page spread which encourages a creative response through speaking and listening. Whether it be a story map, flow chart, game or poster it stimulates discussion and helps provide evidence for comprehension. This, plus the notes to support reading at the back of each book, encourages a thorough exploration of the book, which enriches the material and the whole experience. This includes practical guidance on reading strategies and creative activities, plus discussion prompts to embed learning, develop higher-order thinking skills and ensure the reading process is always reinforced with meaning.

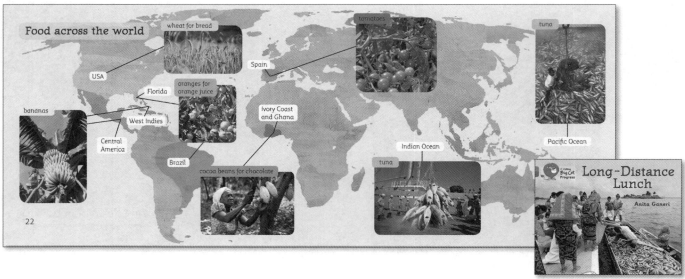

Every child has a right of access to the whole curriculum

Regardless of reading ability, struggling readers ought to have opportunities to read, albeit in less detail and complexity, material which is relevant to the work of the rest of the class, so that they can be included in the wider learning. This is a challenging ideal but here are a few Progress examples:

History: *Animals in War*; *Top Secret*; *Fire in the Sky*; *When Rosa Parks Met Martin Luther King, Junior*; *Growing up in Wartime*; *Winkie's War*; *The Deadly Monster*; *Thin Ice*
Geography: *Long-Distance Lunch*; *Natural Disasters*
Science: *Muscles*
PE: *The Modern Pentathlon*

One of the strengths of Progress is in matching the themes, topics and genres of the books to what is relevant and meaningful to 7–11 year olds.

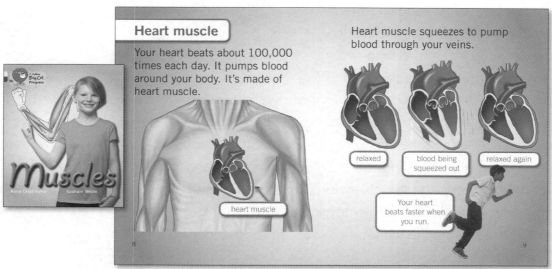

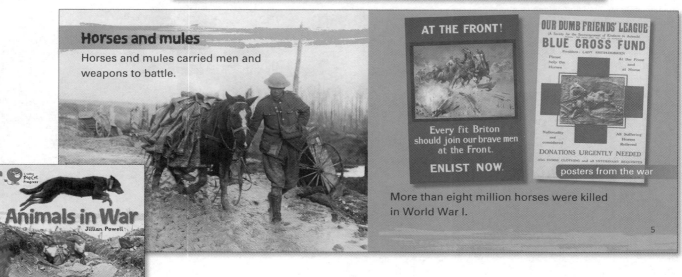

Only the best for struggling and reluctant readers

The best books are those which capture the imagination and interest of inexperienced readers of any age and the Progress strand provides such books with the right text at the right level. They are exciting and dynamic reading resources. Often it is the case that some children have "slipped through the net" and failed to learn to read to a satisfactory level for their age. But do remember that it's perfectly normal in developmental terms for some children to struggle with reading up to the age of nine, so avoid labelling them. Nevertheless they still need the motivation to tackle a wide variety of interesting and absorbing texts in order to maintain and

sustain their literacy development. Reluctant or disengaged readers may have learnt to read but have decided it's not for them. Consequently, they have fallen behind because they have had insufficient practice: as the psycholinguist Frank Smith said, you "learn to read by reading". Again these children need reading material which inspires and captivates and which rewards the considerable effort they put into accomplishing it. In short, both struggling and reluctant readers need access to books which they *want* to read and which will create "readers for life".

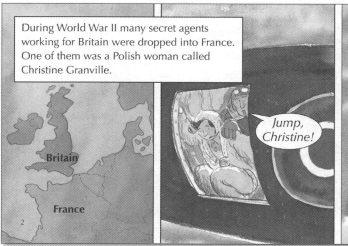

Boys, in particular, need books which capture their interests

It is widely acknowledged that boys are more likely than girls to be struggling or reluctant readers. The reasons are many and varied and include gender stereotypes, early reading experiences at home and in school as well as group pressures.

Whilst Progress is aimed at both boys and girls, there are plenty of titles which will particularly appeal to boys in terms of subject matter and frequency of male protagonists with whom they can identify. Research shows that many boys prefer reading non-fiction and Progress, along with the rest of the Collins Big Cat series, offers an unparalleled amount of factual books. However, it's important to acknowledge that not all boys like the same things, and Progress provides a huge variety of themes and topics for every reader.

Boys will not only find exciting topics to choose from, but they will also be able to read them.

BMX stands for bicycle motocross.

Olympic BMX
Charlotte Guillain

Riders race around tracks on special bikes.

3

Cool Cars
John Foster

Racing cars and bangers
These cars race at more than 300 kilometres per hour.

Formula One racing cars

There are many crashes when bangers race.

6

7

All children have the right to "find themselves in a book"

An important, perhaps the most important, joy of reading comes from the way we get inside the skin of the characters or situations we read about – they are held as a mirror reflecting our own lives and feelings. Years ago a researcher attempted to describe which activities were most likely to foster the development of empathy amongst undergraduates, and it came as no surprise that top of the list was reading fiction. Opportunities for children to empathise with characters may be found in Progress titles such as *Angel House* or *Seal Skull*.

Parents/carers have a role to play too

You can feel confident that Progress books will be enjoyed by parents/carers and children alike. When advising adults on the best ways to support boys' reading, we should stress the desirability of male involvement either as role models by being seen to read themselves or as partners in the shared reading process. Very often parents/carers are bored by the books their children bring home from school, but not with Progress!

Cliff Moon
M.Ed. Reading Consultant

Progress at a glance

Texts are presented specifically for struggling readers, designed across the spread and supported by imagery for accessibility and manageability.

The text used is expertly levelled to ensure readability.

The design is mature enough to allow struggling readers to feel pride in their reading.

Strong, varied imagery supports the text, providing picture cues as well as plenty of speaking and listening opportunities for extended exploration and topic expansion.

Gas masks

Everyone had to carry a gas mask in case of poison gas attacks.

a poster from 1940

Hitler will send no warning — so always carry your gas mask

ISSUED BY THE MINISTRY OF HOME SECURITY

6

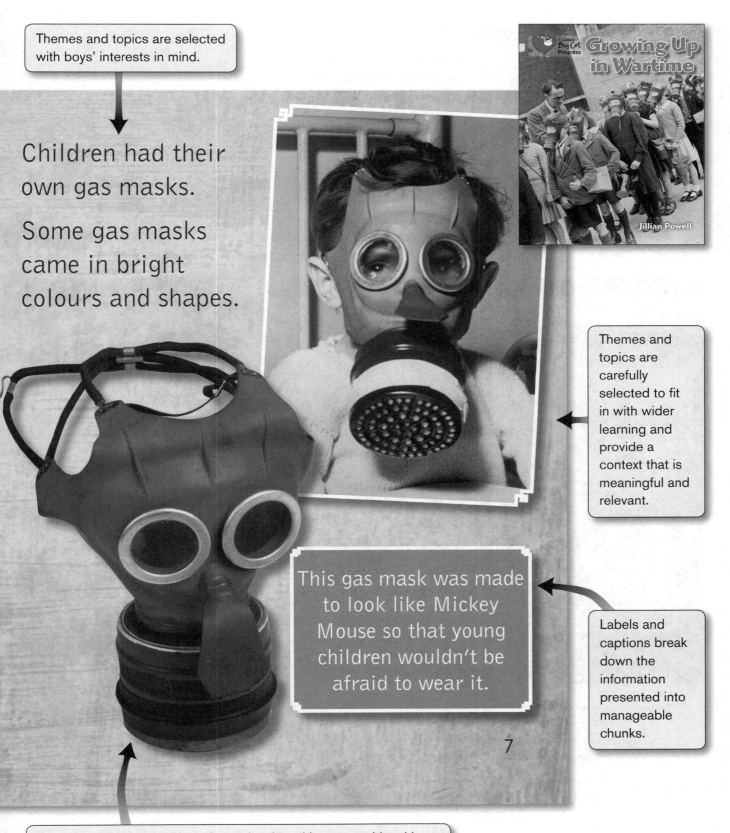

Themes and topics are selected with boys' interests in mind.

Children had their own gas masks.

Some gas masks came in bright colours and shapes.

Growing Up in Wartime

Jillian Powell

Themes and topics are carefully selected to fit in with wider learning and provide a context that is meaningful and relevant.

This gas mask was made to look like Mickey Mouse so that young children wouldn't be afraid to wear it.

Labels and captions break down the information presented into manageable chunks.

7

Many non-fiction books have been developed in partnership with organisations such as Imperial War Museums to provide exceptional texts and wonderful images exclusively to Collins Big Cat.

Reader response activity

Each book has a unique reader response activity at the end of it. This enables you to check children's comprehension through speaking and listening in response to the spread. The wide range of activities, from storyboards to flow charts, maps to charts provides the perfect tool for recall to ensure children have understood what they've read.

An entirely oral device, the reader response page provides enormous speaking and listening opportunities.

This page provides an ideal opportunity to develop higher-order thinking skills such as inference and deduction.

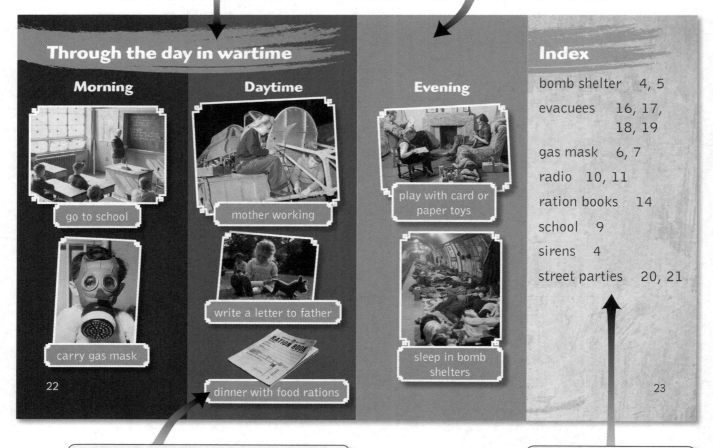

Through the day in wartime

Morning

go to school

carry gas mask

22

Daytime

mother working

write a letter to father

dinner with food rations

Evening

play with card or paper toys

sleep in bomb shelters

Index

bomb shelter   4, 5

evacuees   16, 17, 18, 19

gas mask   6, 7

radio   10, 11

ration books   14

school   9

sirens   4

street parties   20, 21

23

The visual aids enable children to revisit the text demonstrating their understanding.

Indexes and glossaries familiarise children with non-fiction text features, and ensure the book is accessible.

Ideas for reading at your fingertips

At the back of every Collins Big Cat reading book is a double-page spread of Ideas for reading specific to each title. It provides practical support for teaching reading as well as exciting, creative activities to ensure comprehension and development skills such as speaking and listening and higher-order thinking skills.

Learning objectives highlight the learning outcomes of each book. Reading objectives correspond with the text band. All other objectives correspond with the interest band.

Curriculum links highlight the book's relevance to wider learning.

High frequency words help you monitor the child's acquisition of key vocabulary.

Interest words highlight new, topic-relevant vocabulary.

 ## Ideas for reading
Written by Gillian Howell
Primary Literacy Consultant

Learning objectives: *(reading objectives correspond with Green band; all other objectives correspond with Diamond band)* use phonics to read unknown words; appraise a text quickly, deciding on its value/quality/usefulness; understand underlying themes, causes and points of view; improvise using a range of drama strategies and conventions to explore themes such as hopes, fears, desires

Curriculum links: History: What was it like for children in the Second World War?

High frequency words: of, up, the, for, six, from, to, it, lives, at, home, and, school, many, were, in, got, that, when, they, had, take, a, some, on, their, came, made, look, like, so, that, wouldn't, be, way, them, was, by, went, out, girl, her, going, over, if, there, no, but, new, or, as, ran, goods, people, with, what, could, five, called, May

Interest words: wartime, bomb, shelters, sirens, enemy, London Underground, gas mask, poison, aeroplanes, programme, comics, machines, weapons, hopscotch, rations, coupons, evacuees, abroad

Resources: paper, pens, pencils, paint, whiteboard

Word count: 420

Getting started

Ask the children to say what they already know about the lives of children in wartime. Read the title together and look at the front cover. Ask the children what the photograph on the cover shows and what the children are wearing.

- Ask the children to read the contents page aloud. If children struggle with any of the words, e.g. rations, remind them to think of other words they know with similar letter strings e.g. *tion* in *mention*. Remind them to use their phonic knowledge to chop words into sounds, and then blend the sounds together.

- Ask the children which section in the contents page might give them information that is furthest from their own lives and why. Note their responses on the whiteboard.

Reading and responding

- Ask the children to read the text quietly. Listen to the children as they read and prompt as necessary.

- As they read, pause and ask the children to say what information they can find in the photographs to help them understand the text. For example on p2, ask the children to read the newspaper headlines. What extra information do these headlines give them?

- Ask the children at each section to give their own opinion about how they think children felt during the war. On pp6–7, do they think the children enjoyed wearing gas masks? How would they feel if they had to wear one?

Returning to the book

- Look together at pp22–23. Invite the children to describe to a partner what the information shows. Ask them to compare each point with their own lives.

- Refer back to the whiteboard notes to see if the children still agree with their first ideas about which aspects of wartime life differ from their own.

- Discuss why children were sent away from the towns. Ask them to give reasons why the countryside would have been a safer place for children.

- Ask the children to say what they have learnt about growing up in wartime from reading this book. Do they think any other information should be included and why? Ask them to say how they would recommend this book to others.

Checking and moving on

- Ask the children to work in pairs and prepare a short role-play about a chosen chapter. Invite pairs to perform their role-plays to the rest of the group in the chapter sequence from the book.

- Ask the children to look at the posters illustrated in the text. Ask them to design and illustrate a new wartime poster that gives advice to children about the war on one topic that has been discussed.

When the Siren Sounds, Take Shelter

Bomb shelters save lives – always know where your nearest one is before you leave home.

Reading more

Angel House (Green/Band 5, Diamond/Band 17) another Green/Diamond book within Collins Big Cat progress.

Getting started
Activities and discussion prompts engage the reader in the topic and themes of the book.

Reading and responding
Practical support for developing reading skills and strategies.

Returning to the book
Creative ideas and discussion prompts to stimulate recall of the text, explore the themes and develop higher-order thinking skills, including guidance on getting the most out of the reader response activity.

Checking and moving on
More extensive activities to take learning beyond the book, including writing and whole-class topic work.

Reading more
Relevant further reading to keep children engaged in reading.

Structure chart

Interest level	Readability and National Curriculum Level
Copper **Band 12** **Year 3/P4** **Age 7–8**	**Yellow, Band 3, Year 1/P2** National Curriculum Level: Working within Level 1 Curriculum for Excellence Level: First
	Blue, Band 4, Year 1/P2 National Curriculum Level: Working within Level 1 Curriculum for Excellence Level: First
	Green, Band 5, Year 1/P2 National Curriculum Level: Working within Level 1 Curriculum for Excellence Level: First
Ruby **Band 14** **Year 4/P5** **Age 8–9**	**Yellow, Band 3, Year 1/P2** National Curriculum Level: Working within Level 1 Curriculum for Excellence Level: First
	Blue, Band 4, Year 1/P2 National Curriculum Level: Working within Level 1 Curriculum for Excellence Level: First
	Green, Band 5, Year 1/P2 National Curriculum Level: Working within Level 1 Curriculum for Excellence Level: First
Sapphire **Band 16** **Year 5/P6** **Age 9–10**	**Yellow, Band 3, Year 1/P2** National Curriculum Level: Working within Level 1 Curriculum for Excellence Level: First
	Blue, Band 4, Year 1/P2 National Curriculum Level: Working within Level 1 Curriculum for Excellence Level: First
	Green, Band 5, Year 1/P2 National Curriculum Level: Working within Level 1 Curriculum for Excellence Level: First
Diamond **Band 17** **Year 6/P7** **Age 10–11**	**Yellow, Band 3, Year 1/P2** National Curriculum Level: Working within Level 1 Curriculum for Excellence Level: First
	Blue, Band 4, Year 1/P2 National Curriculum Level: Working within Level 1 Curriculum for Excellence Level: First
	Green, Band 5, Year 1/P2 National Curriculum Level: Working within Level 1 Curriculum for Excellence Level: First

Titles		Teacher support
Fiction	**Non-fiction**	
Mission Mars A science-fiction story	**Cool Cars** A non-fiction book	
The Dolphin King A story from another culture	**Tigers in Trouble** A non-fiction book	
The Deadly Monster A graphic novel	**Natural Disasters** An information book	
In the Game A graphic novel	**Olympic BMX** A non-fiction report	
Dinner with a Pirate A story from another culture	**World's Deadliest Creatures** An information book	
Zara and the Fairy Godbrother A fantasy story	**Long-Distance Lunch** A non-fiction report	
Top Secret A graphic novel set in the past	**Muscles** An information book	Collins **Big Cat Progress Handbook**
Seal Skull A mystery story	**The Modern Pentathlon** An information book	
Winkie's War A graphic novel set in the past	**Amazing Escapes** A non-fiction recount	
Thin Ice An adventure book	**When Rosa Parks Met Martin Luther King, Junior** A non-fiction recount	
Fire in the Sky A graphic novel set in the past	**Animals in War** A non-chronological report	
Angel House A fantasy story	**Growing up in Wartime** A non-chronological report	

The books

Yellow/Band 3   Year 1/P2   National Curriculum level: Working within Level 1
Curriculum for Excellence Level: First

Fiction

Interest level

Copper Band 12 Year 3/P4 Age 7–8

Mission Mars

By Anne Curtis

The Star Ship Orca is taking off on a mission to find a new planet for the people of Earth. First stop: Mars. But will the crew find anything there except rocks and sand?

Curriculum links
Science: Light and shadows

Text type
A science-fiction story

High frequency words
to, a, new, for, the, people, of, we, have, off, our, in, your, last, good, do, home, all, now, on, there, no, live, here, but, look, been, and

---

Ruby Band 14 Year 4/P5 Age 8–9

In the Game

By Katy Coope

Dan and Sara are bored. There's nothing to do, so they're sitting in the park playing a computer game – but little do they know what adventures are happening right behind them …

Curriculum links
ICT: Exploring simulations

Text type
A graphic novel

High frequency words
what, are, you, me, too, I, love, this, I'm, get, here, yes, we, did, it, not, much, is, here, home, see

---

Sapphire Band 16 Year 5/P6 Age 9–10

Top Secret

By Mick Manning and Brita Granström

During World War II, many spies were dropped from Britain into France to help fight the Nazis. One of them was a woman called Christine Granville, who risked her life to save her comrades. Follow her incredible true story.

Curriculum links
History: What can we learn about recent history by studying the life of a famous person?

Text type
A graphic novel set in the past

High frequency words
many, for, were, one, of, them, was, a, called, jump, good, the, had, help, up, they, put, in, days, night, some, dog, but, their, to, boy, our, have, been, got, all, this, for, could, you, as, took, her

---

Diamond Band 17 Year 6/P7 Age 10–11

Thin Ice

By Anne Curtis

Captain Scott travelled to the Antarctic in 1901 – the first man in the world ever to go there. Join one man as he follows in Scott's footsteps and understands why the Antarctic is so important to us.

Curriculum links
History: What can we learn about recent history by studying the life of a famous person?; Geography: Weather around the world

Text type
An adventure book

High frequency words
we, to, the, like, in, were, when, a, I, my, for, is, this, where, lived, about, his, and, what, he, did, made, on, back, home, had, here, of, but, now, one, day, will, be, must

---

Yellow/Band 3   Year 1/P2

Non-fiction

Cool Cars

By John Foster

Some cars are big and powerful, while others are very small. Some can even fly or float on water! Find out about some of the world's coolest and most unusual cars in this highly photographic information book.

Curriculum links
Design and Technology: Vehicles; Science: Forces and movement

Text type
A non-fiction book

High frequency words
old, had, three, this, had, a, of, these, can, go, at, more, than, so, that, it, has, to, down, one, there, are, many, when, some, make, five, made, with, and, on, is, as, an, for

Olympic BMX

By Charlotte Guillain

Riding a BMX, or Bicycle Motocross, is very different to riding an ordinary road bike. Find out all the differences, the tricks, techniques and amazing skills that go into making a great Olympic BMX competitor.

Curriculum links
P.E.: Outdoor and adventurous activities

Text type
A non-fiction report

High frequency words
some, do, one, eight, has, out, what, how, be

Muscles

By Anna Claybourne

What is a muscle? How does it work? Why is it so important? Find out the answers to all of these questions in this information book, filled with detailed diagrams and photographs.

Curriculum links
Science: Keeping healthy

Text type
An information book

High frequency words
your, one, that, two, three, have, over, there, about, made, when, time(s), so, some, too

When Rosa Parks Met Martin Luther King, Junior

By Zoë Clarke

In some parts of America in the 1950s, white people and black people were treated very differently. Rosa Parks and Martin Luther King publicly fought against this – but in very different ways. This is the powerful and inspiring story of how they stood up for racial equality.

Curriculum links
Citizenship: Living in a diverse world; History: What can we learn about recent history by studying the life of a famous person?

Text type
A non-fiction recount

High frequency words
did, not, that, black, people, white, should, be, how, were, way, if, got, had, who, her, took, many, with, one, them, over, so

Blue/Band 4   Year 1/P2   National Curriculum level: Working within Level 1
Curriculum for Excellence Level: First

Fiction

Interest level

Copper Band 12 Year 3/P4 Age 7–8

The Dolphin King

By Saviour Pirotta

Jean and his friends are fishermen. Jean throws a spear at a passing dolphin to show his strength and suddenly the crew are swept into a terrible storm. Will Jean be able to make up for his mistakes?

Curriculum links
Citizenship: Animals and us

Text type
A story from another culture

High frequency words
from, his, were, will, be, than, as, out, take, down, there, must, him, that, your, again, took, back, had

Ruby Band 14 Year 4/P5 Age 8–9

Dinner with a Pirate

By Saviour Pirotta

When Pedro the fisherman catches a big swordfish, he decides to share his meal with a man in the local prison – a captured pirate. But when Pedro himself is later captured by a pirate gang, he finds his generosity hasn't been forgotten.

Curriculum links
Citizenship: Choices

Text type
A story from another culture

High frequency words
one, good, with, made, took, want, his, who, had, been, him, many, by, man, came, new, that, must, be, when, out, an, your, home, but, now, have

Sapphire Band 16 Year 5/P6 Age 9–10

Seal Skull

By Anne Curtis

A boy takes home a seal skull that he finds at the beach. It has dark, empty eyes that stare back at him. Now a storm is brewing and his room is filled with shadows – will he be able to calm the storm?

Curriculum links
Citizenship: Animals and us

Text type
A mystery story

High frequency words
water, white, with, bed, because, last, night, saw, were, when, there('s), must, take, back, make, as

Diamond Band 17 Year 6/P7 Age 10–11

Fire in the Sky

By Mick Manning and Brita Granström

Discover the incredible true story of Sergeant Norman Jackson, who had survived 30 missions when his plane was hit over enemy territory in 1945. Under fire and travelling at 200mph he climbed onto the wing, attempting to put out the blaze.

Curriculum links
History: What are we remembering on Remembrance Day?

Text type
A graphic novel set in the past

High frequency words
in, by, five, had, over, but, many, of, his, been, one, night, was, an, a, in, the, it, to, put, out, lives, he, on, with, him, off, I, must, with, my, you, four, your, for

Blue/Band 4 Year 1/P2 National Curriculum level: Working within Level 1
Curriculum for Excellence Level: First

Non-fiction

Tigers in Trouble

By Louise Spilsbury

Once, there were 100,000 tigers in the world, but now these beautiful creatures are under threat of extinction. Find out the reasons for the decrease in tiger numbers, and what we can do to change it.

Curriculum links
Citizenship: Animals and us

Text type
A non-fiction book

High frequency words
are, the, of, all, big, cats, there, were, once, in, now, just, many, live, with, trees, and, they, can, people, down, to, new, houses, and, their, have, when, on, no, who, put, out, for, some, homes, make, from, help, up

World's Deadliest Creatures

By Anna Claybourne

What are the most dangerous animals in the world? Take a closer look at some very poisonous, venomous and deadly animals.

Curriculum links
Citizenship: Animals and us; Geography: Habitats

Text type
An information book

High frequency words
out, very, or, not, water, some, but, has, your, with, their, blue, so, half, three, if, one(s), them

The Modern Pentathlon

By Zoë Clarke

At the 2012 Olympics, the modern pentathlon will be 100 years old. Find out what events are included in the pentathlon and the extraordinary skills needed to compete in this challenging event.

Curriculum links
Citizenship: Taking part; PE: Athletic activities

Text type
An information book

High frequency words
out, what, how, be, there, five, take(s), one, with, then, not, more, jump, time, off, down, have, green, last, two

Animals in War

By Jillian Powell and Imperial War Museums

From pigeons and elephants to parachuting dogs – millions of animals helped in both world wars. With fascinating photographs from the archives of the Imperial War Museums, find out about the animals that were involved and their bravery in the face of battle.

Curriculum links
History: What was it like to live here in the past?; Citizenship: Animals and us

Text type
A non-chronological report

High frequency words
did, in, they, was, that, out, and, to, more, than, eight, were, too, could, people, by, home, when, not, be, a, on, its, up, it, dogs, too, their, or, from, with, as, if, there, good, of, very, the, this, some, but, many

Green/Band 5   Year 1/P2

National Curriculum level: Working within Level 1
Curriculum for Excellence Level: First

Fiction

Interest level

Copper Band 12 Year 3/P4 Age 7–8

The Deadly Monster

By Linda Chapman

Jack and Sam think their school trip to the museum is boring, until they see a glowing statue ... Finding themselves whisked away to fight a deadly monster, suddenly Ancient Greece doesn't seem so dull after all.

Curriculum links
History: Who were the Ancient Greeks?

Text type
A graphic novel

High frequency words
but, back, him, were, if, one, more, that, what, help, where, your, must, be, by, or, will, from, his, took, ran, how, could, had, boy(s), have, as, after

Ruby Band 14 Year 4/P5 Age 8–9

Zara and the Fairy Godbrother

By Margaret Ryan

When Zara wishes for a new dress for the school party she doesn't expect to see a fairy godbrother land in her room, especially when he tries to "text-a-spell" with unpredictable results! Will Zara ever get her dream dress?

Curriculum links
ICT: Writing for different audiences

Text type
A fantasy story

High frequency words
school, but, want, her, old, what, that, too, much, have, had, new, one, boy, your, who, do, about, not, took, out, his, don't, bed, can't, got, again, must, be, some, girl(s), were, very, just, could

Sapphire Band 16 Year 5/P6 Age 9–10

Winkie's War

By Mick Manning and Brita Granström

Follow the true story of Winkie, a carrier pigeon in World War II whose crew crash-landed in the sea. All hopes rested with Winkie as she battled through the elements to reach help – but would she be able to lead them back to her crew?

Curriculum links
Citizenship: Animals and us

Text type
A graphic novel set in the past

High frequency words
was, as, a, if, they, at, it, eight, to, on, its, and, way, home, all, she, for, had, her, what's, their, over, the, were, for, help, I, our, but, could, back, day, by, how, old, girl, this, him, where, see, them, lives

Diamond Band 17 Year 6/P7 Age 10–11

Angel House

By Anne Curtis

He doesn't fit in at school; they don't understand him there. But in Angel House he feels stronger – he feels free. Follow one boy who is discovering his own emotions as he makes his way through a house that is full of secrets of its own.

Curriculum links
Geography: Weather around the world

Text type
A fantasy story

High frequency words
house, there, times, don't, be, have, an, old, where, live, has, one, with, more, when, from, as, white, out, if, not

Green/Band 5

Year 1/P2

National Curriculum level: Working within Level 1
Curriculum for Excellence Level: First

Non-fiction

Natural Disasters

Adrian Bradbury

Find out about the natural disasters people face around the world, what effect they have on towns and cities and how we can help to protect people from them. Packed with fact files and maps showing disaster spots, find out all you need to know about hurricanes, earthquakes, volcanoes and tsunamis.

Curriculum links
Geography: Weather around the world

Text type
An information book

High frequency words
what, how, do, or, be, but, people, over, have, their, home(s), there, five, from, out, first, time, some, then, again, after, where, made, when, way, down, one, an, after, many, may, water, more, over, that, help

Long-Distance Lunch

By Anita Ganeri

Where does the food in your lunch-box come from? How far has it travelled? Find out where bananas are grown, where tuna is found and how chocolate is made.

Curriculum links
Geography: Connecting ourselves to the world;
Citizenship: Living in a diverse world

Text type
A non-fiction report

High frequency words
have, where, your, from, how, has, made, make, people, put, that, green, yellow, as, then, with, orange, called, out, some, by, be, much, us, who, were, their

Amazing Escapes

By John Foster

Read the miraculous true-life survival stories from across the world of lucky people who escaped dangerous situations, such as being bitten by a shark, lost at sea or trapped in an avalanche.

Curriculum links
Citizenship: People who help us

Text type
A non-fiction recount

High frequency words
from, out, by, be, some, people, have, or, but, one, girl, nine, saw, her, him, his, three, boy(s), got, their, ran, had, with, them, after, man, five, an, because, could, were, these, time, last

Growing Up in Wartime

By Jillian Powell and Imperial War Museums

Find out what life was like for the children growing up during World War II. With photographs straight from the archives of the Imperial War Museums, find out about rationing, schooling, evacuation and how the daily lives of children were affected by the war.

Curriculum links
History: What was it like for children in the Second World War?

Text type
A non-chronological report

High frequency words
of, up, the, for, six, from, to, it, lives, at, home, and, school, many, were, in, got, that, when, they, had, take, a, some, on, their, came, made, look, like, so, that, wouldn't, be, way, them, was, by, went, out, girl, her, going, over, if, there, no, but, new, or, as, ran, goods, people, with, what, could, five, called, May

Meet the authors

Mick Manning and Brita Granström

We have been writing and illustrating children's books together for about 18 years. Our awards include the Smarties Silver Prize, the TES Award and we are four times winners of The English Association Non-Fiction Award. We have four sons of our own and often visit school classrooms too, so we appreciate that books for all readers must be captivating. We love mixing up words and pictures in exciting ways, including comic strip and fact boxes to add layers of information.

Anne Curtis

I began my publishing career as an illustrator, but now enjoy writing more than drawing – which is saying something, as I really love drawing! The best times, though, are when I can do both. I've won awards for my work, including the ERA "Best Education Book".

Linda Chapman

I've been writing for 14 years and have written over 150 books, including the best-selling *My Secret Unicorn* series. Before becoming a full-time writer I trained as a teacher and then worked as a tutor, particularly helping children who had problems with reading or writing. The biggest compliment I can have is for a child to say they'd never read a book until they picked up one of my titles, and now they have read the whole series. There's nothing better than feeling I've helped a child to become a reader!

Zoë Clarke

I am a children's book editor and writer. I have been editing children's books for 15 years, and in the last two years I have written five books, both fiction and non-fiction.

Margaret Ryan

I'm a former primary school teacher and have written about a hundred children's books, some of them specifically for struggling readers. I won a Scottish Arts Council award for *The Queen's Birthday Hat* and Richard and Judy picked up the first in the *Roodica the Rude* series for the launch of their Children's Book Club. I often do author visits to libraries and once had a boy take my hand and ask me to show him where my books were, because he thought he really might be able to read them. A magic moment.

Jillian Powell

I started writing stories when I was four, drawing pictures for them in crayons. At the last count, I've written over 280 books for children, including information books and stories for struggling readers. They include stories about everything from ghosts and scarecrows to pirates and robots.

On *Growing up in Wartime* and *Animals in War* I worked with Imperial War Museums. Using photos straight from their archives and expertise from the museums' education department, we were able to develop two new titles on wartime from exciting new perspectives.

John Foster

As a teacher, I've always been interested in helping children to become readers. My grandson Louis is fascinated by cars, so I picked his brains and that's how *Cool Cars* came to be written. I wrote the true stories of *Amazing Escapes* because they are so incredible they can't help but capture a child's interest. I've written about 150 books on all kinds of subjects, including UFOs, football and the Olympic Games. I've also written 12 books of my own poetry, and have visited over 500 schools to perform my poems.

Anita Ganeri

I was born in India, but grew up in Britain. Books have always played a very large part in my life, and my first job was in children's publishing in London. When I moved to Yorkshire, I took up writing full-time and have never looked back. I've written more than 400 books, including the award-winning *Horrible Geography* series. It gives me huge pleasure to explain often-complex subjects in a way that is informative, fun and accessible to readers of all abilities.

Louise Spilsbury

I've been writing children's non-fiction on a huge range of subjects, from art to animals and health to history, for over 20 years. Many of the 200-plus books I've worked on have been for primary-school-age children and struggling readers. Having worked with struggling readers in primary school classrooms, I know how engaging, carefully-targeted texts can inspire a child to keep going and to finish a book.

Katy Coope

I had my first book published when I was 17, and made a second book during my A-levels before going on to write *How to Make Manga Characters* for Collins Big Cat, which was shortlisted for the Society of Authors Educational Writers Prize. *In the Game* is my fourth book. I teach as well as writing and drawing, and often end up using manga and comics to reach out to children who aren't connecting very well with the rest of their education.

Saviour Pirotta

I was born on the island of Malta but moved to England after finishing my education. Before becoming a writer, I worked as a chef, a storyteller and a postman. My career with the post office ended when I was bitten by a dog. I've got a large tattoo on my left leg to hide the scar. I love visiting schools and talking to children who struggle with their reading, using the power of oral storytelling to inspire them.

Adrian Bradbury

I've been a teacher for 32 years, and taught English as a Foreign Language overseas for 12 of those years in Europe, the Far East and the Middle East. In 2006 I gave up a Deputy Headship to write humorous educational football books for boys, setting up my own company and publishing three books in this area. I now teach part-time and write stories and non-fiction texts to develop reading skills, whilst also giving talks in schools about writing and publishing.

Charlotte Guillain

I've been writing and editing children's books for over ten years. I've written close to a hundred books about subjects as wide-ranging as vampires, outer space, punk music and spies. I try to spend as much time as possible in schools talking to children about what they want to read and particularly enjoy the challenge of engaging struggling and reluctant readers. Before I became a writer I taught English as a Foreign Language in various parts of the world.

Anna Claybourne

I have been writing children's non-fiction (and some fiction) for over 15 years, and have published over 150 books. I specialise in science and nature, and have written a number of books for struggling readers. My books have won and been nominated for various awards including the TES Information Book Award, the Blue Peter Book Awards and the Children's Choice Book Awards in the US. I'm a passionate believer in the importance of science and factual books, and I've seen how they can capture children's attention.

2 Identifying struggling readers

If a child struggles with reading, there are probably two main reasons:

1) They find it difficult to match letter sounds and shapes and put them together to make words and sentences.

2) They think reading is boring and prefer to do other things instead.

This means that those who can't read, won't read, which makes the problem worse. And those who just won't read fall behind and can become one of those who can't read.

The causes

Not all struggling readers are the same. There are different types of struggling reader and reasons why they struggle, which are important to identify in relation to working towards the most appropriate support. Readers who struggle may fall into one or several of these categories.

- **Decoding**
  When children have difficulty in decoding text, their reading becomes slow and laboured. This affects their comprehension as they lose the flow of the text. They then lose interest in the story or subject and the difficulty in decoding then affects their self-image as a reader.

- **Comprehension**
  Children who have problems with comprehension may have little or no prior knowledge of the context and are unable to make connections between different elements within the text. They may struggle with short-term memory which also affects their ability to make connections.

- **Attention**
  Children who have short attention spans may begin reading with some level of enthusiasm but fairly quickly lose interest. They can be distracted by the sounds and activities of others around them or feel they have spent long enough reading and other media competes for their attention. They may discover that they do not relate to the characters or content of the text and so lose interest.

- **Memory**

Working memory and long-term memory are important elements in both decoding and comprehension skills. Working memory is the process of retaining information necessary for comprehending that information in the moment. Children who struggle with reading have to keep far more in their working memory than pupils for whom decoding has become an automatic process. This means that when they encounter something new on one page, they may struggle to decode a word they have already read on the previous page. Long-term memory is a store of everything we know about, have experienced and can do. Children with poor long-term memory struggle with comprehension because they are unable to make connections with what they are reading and their own experiences.

- **Motivation**

Struggling readers may feel that reading is not "cool". They may have a lack of role-models, particularly male, who demonstrate an excitement and eagerness about reading. They have an image of readers as being boring or "geeky" people, or something only adults do. They may see reading as a solitary occupation and prefer more social activities. They feel the content of the stories or non-fiction texts at school have no relevance to their own lives.

The symptoms

Just as there are many reasons why children become unwilling to read, there are many behaviours that demonstrate this reluctance. When these behaviours are repeated regularly this can be a sign that the child is a struggling reader.

- They regularly make excuses not to read such as the book is too easy, too hard, boring or babyish, or they urgently need to do other things such as sharpen their pencils or go to the toilet.
- Their reading is a slow, laborious process. They stop more often than eager readers, looking away from the page more frequently.
- They look over the page to find words they recognise and have memorised while they guess and skip words they cannot decode.
- They may automatically read a word on one line and then be completely baffled by the same word when it occurs later on the same page or later in the text.

Other children may simply not read because they don't want to or can't be bothered. They are more interested in other things. This doesn't mean that they do no reading whatsoever. They probably read emails, text messages, websites, magazines or comics and text in the environment. They just see no pleasure in reading at school. This may be because the material given to them to read is of no interest to them or that they dislike reading aloud through shyness or embarrassment.

Diagnostics

If the behaviour pattern signals an unwillingness to read, the next step is to drill down and try to diagnose the problem. The following questions can assist you in identifying when to step in and give extra support:

Does the child have a negative attitude to reading?

Does the child have an unwillingness to participate?

Does the child have low confidence in his or her abilities?

Does the child make excuses not to read?

Does the child see no point or value in reading?

Does the child give up easily?

Does the child skip words and fail to self-correct?

Does the child fail to remember words that they had seen on the previous page?

Does the child guess at unknown words?

When the answer is yes to any of these questions, it is important to engage with the child to identify the underlying cause and provide the appropriate support as soon as possible. When the reluctance of these children to take part in literacy activities is interpreted as defiance or laziness, their underlying reading problem may not be identified, and it can become entrenched with a detrimental effect on wider learning.

Getting boys reading

Lots of research has shown that the majority of struggling readers are boys. Researchers have found that many boys stop reading because they do not see practical applications for reading. Many boys tend to look for immediate uses for what they learn. When they read texts with universal themes or fiction, which has no immediate relevance to their own lives, they fail to see the purpose in reading.

Providing the right books is vital. Identifying boys' interests and suggesting books they would like can help them see the relevance of reading.

Content and choice

Collins Big Cat Progress has been designed specifically to appeal to boys, while the topics and content will also be appropriate for girl readers. Girls don't mind reading fiction where the main protagonist is male, but the opposite tends to apply to boys. Although Collins Big Cat Progress does have some female protagonists, the majority are male. Non-fiction topics have been specifically chosen to appeal to boys' interests. They present incidents and people who are inspirational, with content that deals with individual struggles, overcoming challenges and dealing with emotions.

Suitable books for struggling readers need to be high interest, non-fiction with relevant topics, graphic novels, exciting illustrations, and have believable characters that children can identify with in order to compete with the highly illustrated, fast paced computer games, film and television that children are exposed to at home. All of this has been included in the series.

Whenever possible, allow boys to choose their own books. They can be reluctant to read a book because the illustrations or cover doesn't appeal to them, or simply because it looks too long or babyish. When they choose their own books, it gives them the opportunity to "buy into" the process of reading and have the satisfaction of "finding themselves" in a book. This can boost their self-esteem and change their perceptions about themselves as readers.

The importance of role-models

Boys have a lack of good role-models for reading. Enthusiasm can be infectious, so always model reading with enthusiasm. If you can show the children that you are excited about reading, it will gradually rub off on them. Plenty of positive reinforcement and praise will also give struggling readers a sense of achievement and improve their self-esteem.

3 Collins Big Cat Progress in practice

Thinking about how to manage reading sessions with struggling readers is important. There are benefits to both group work and a one-to-one approach.

Working in small groups allows children to share ideas and impressions of books with each other, which enhances their comprehension skills. Teachers can ask open questions to generate discussion, make tentative comments such as "I wonder why ..." that can encourage children to ask their own questions about a text. Children are also given the opportunity to compare their own thinking with others in the group and learn from each other. Working with a group enables teachers to make maximum use of their teaching time. Working with individual children can be valuable when a child needs extra help in using a particular strategy that doesn't apply to the rest of the group or in monitoring an individual child's progress. Monitoring progress has a two-fold purpose – to guide the instructional needs of the pupil and to track the pupil's progress towards becoming a fluent reader.

Collins Big Cat Progress targets older struggling readers by providing simple texts on topics of a more mature nature. This is designed, not only to give their reading meaning and relevance and help children to engage with the content, but to facilitate responses appropriate to their chronological age rather than their actual reading age, and make use of their higher-order thinking skills and personal life experiences. The depth and complexity of the themes and topics provide valuable areas for discussion, enabling children to make connections between the text and the wider world, encouraging their thinking beyond the book and facilitating cross-curricular work.

Inside the back cover of each of the Collins Big Cat Progress books is a set of teaching notes with ideas and suggestions for creating a successful and comprehensive reading session. Learning objectives are highlighted – for decoding at the children's reading or ability level, but also for other skills such as interpretation, speaking and listening and drama at their chronological level. Embedded in the notes are ways to engage the children before beginning the book, reading strategies to provide practical support as well as discussion points, and speaking and listening ideas to promote exploration of the text, exploration of children's opinions and to enrich learning. There are also wider activities, including writing ideas to take learning beyond the book. The range of literacy and cross-curricular follow-up activities allows for active teaching and learning and addresses a range of learning styles: aural, visual and kinaesthetic.

The notes use a consistent, easy-to-follow structure:

Getting started

Returning to the book

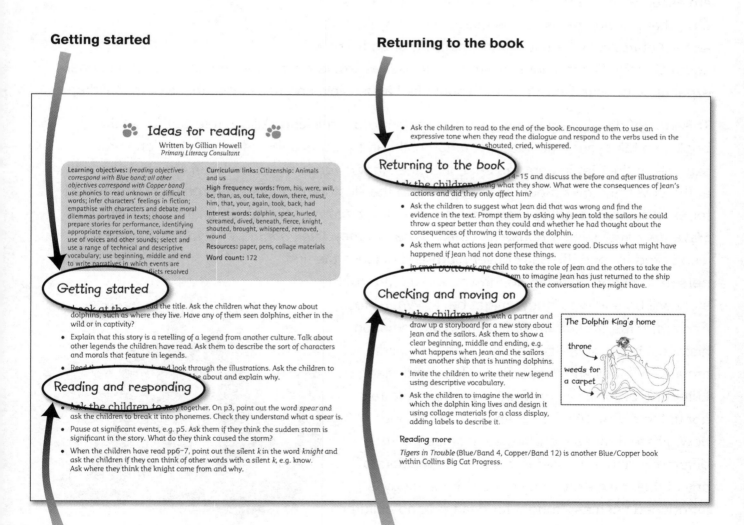

Reading and responding

Checking and moving on

Getting started

Pre-reading activities help children to engage with the book, assist their comprehension and pre-empt difficulties with unknown words. Such activities could be exploring the pictures in the book, introducing vocabulary, discussing the topic or genre, activating prior knowledge, prediction, setting the context and/or a purpose for reading, making connections with other reading and real-life experience.

This is an important stage for all readers, and struggling readers in particular, as it sets the context for reading. For example, the Getting started activities in the *Thin Ice* notes focus on discussing the cover illustration. Pupils are asked where in the world has conditions like this and what it would be like to be there, what they know about Antarctica, where it is and what they already know about Captain Scott. These environmental issues would be beyond the scope and personal experience of Year 1 children, but should feel accessible and relevant to these older children.

This idea of developing age-appropriate higher-order thinking skills is relevant for all the books, so take your time and encourage children to discuss things as you go along. For example in the Getting started section in the *Angel House* notes, children are asked to look at the cover and give a personal response to the illustration. Question prompts are provided for extra support, e.g. *What impression does the picture of the house give about the book? Have they ever seen a house like this? What do they think might be inside?* Children are also asked to read the back cover blurb and discuss the first person "I" usage, thinking about who the narrator of the story will be and who "they" might be. In *When Rosa Parks met Martin Luther King, Junior*, a non-fiction historical book, some context is useful, so children are asked if they know who Rosa Parks and Martin Luther King, Junior were. They're prompted to talk about the civil rights movement in America and how different races were/are sometimes treated differently, and to consider this topic in relation to any of their own experiences. Key phraseology is introduced such as, "fought for change" and children are asked to discuss features of the text type, e.g. past tense verbs, captioned photos and illustrations.

Reading and responding

The texts in Progress and the accompanying teaching notes, specifically the practical Reading and responding section, have been carefully written to allow use of all four of the main reading strategies: phonic, contextual, graphic and syntactic. As struggling readers often have difficulty using one or more of these devices, the substitution of another device to make sense of the text can alleviate the immediate problem, providing a sense of achievement and level of success that keeps the session moving. This also allows teachers to identify and focus on what the particular area of difficulty is and support the acquisition of that skill.

As well as decoding and phonic knowledge, the main problem areas for struggling readers are weak vocabulary, lack of fluency, low self esteem and poor comprehension. Let's look in more detail at each of the key problem areas in turn:

Decoding and phonics

- difficulty matching sounds and letters
- slow and laboured decoding
- difficulty identifying patterns in spelling
- guessing at words based on the first letter or two
- inability to recognise letter patterns in texts, after being taught them

What you can do:
- teach phonics in a systematic and explicit way
- create opportunities to engage children in reading and writing activities that require them to apply the phonics that they have been taught as soon after teaching as possible
- try alternative reading strategies to read tricky words

For example, in the Reading and responding section of the *Olympic BMX* notes children are reminded of their knowledge of sounds and spellings to work out words they are unsure of, and prompted to look for words within words such as "motocross" and "freestyle". In *Zara and the Fairy Godbrother* they're reminded of their phonic and picture cueing skills to work out new words.

Vocabulary

- weak vocabulary
- inability to make connections among words in texts
- inability to find the right word to describe something

What you can do:
- explain important, useful and difficult vocabulary before children read the text. This will help them remember the words and improve comprehension
- encourage children to use new vocabulary orally to help them remember the meaning
- encourage them to use context and picture clues to determine the meanings of words

For example, in *The Modern Pentathlon*, children are asked to describe what the person on the cover is wearing as a Getting Started activity, then in Reading and responding, they are reminded that information can also be found in the photographs and captions. They then describe clothes worn in fencing and show the evidence in the book. They are referred to their original descriptions of the cover and discuss whether they understand the outfit on the cover more now than when they first looked at it. This enables them to use new or tricky vocabulary in response to visual cues, first as an initial response, and later re-using the vocabulary based on greater knowledge and information gained in reading.

Fluency

- frustration when reading aloud because of mistakes
- inability to read with expression
- inability to pause at appropriate times, e.g. between paragraphs

What you can do:

- encourage the child to read simpler texts at an independent reading level aloud to practise fluent reading so that decoding is not an issue
- model reading with expression and encourage the children to copy you
- encourage children to read a passage with a given feeling, e.g. anger, sadness or excitement, to emphasise expression and intonation
- show children how to look for clues in the text, e.g. exclamation marks, that tell how that text should be read

In the Reading and responding section of the *Mission Mars* notes the colon is pointed out so that children can think about how the text following it will be read, e.g. as a list. They're also asked to think about who is speaking the dialogue in the speech bubbles and practise reading those bits with expression. Similarly in *The Dolphin King*, children are encouraged to read the spoken words using an expressive tone, particularly by responding to different reporting clauses, e.g. shouted, cried, whispered.

Self esteem

Low self-esteem may be identified by listening to the things children say about themselves relating to reading, such as:

- I hate reading
- reading is stupid
- there's no point to reading
- I'm stupid – my reading is awful

What you can do:

- show empathy
- explain that learning anything requires practise
- show them the progress they make
- target the child's interests

In actual fact, getting to the end of a book will, in itself, be very rewarding. So just reading a manageable text that feels appropriate will be a huge confidence boost.

Returning to the book

An effective way to improve children's comprehension abilities is to encourage strategies such as predicting, questioning and summarising the texts before, during and after reading. Each of the teaching notes is organised to include these approaches, specifically with older children in mind.

Returning to the book activities focus on reviewing comprehension strategies and revisiting questions from the start of the session. The notes contain suggestions to deepen children's understanding, for discussing author intent and viewpoint, evaluating character, assessing or evaluating information and exploring different forms and styles of writing.

The final problem area for struggling readers is comprehension:

Comprehension

- inability to identify the main ideas in a text
- understands the outcome of a story, but inability to explain how the outcome occurred
- inability to describe the logical sequence of events in a story
- inability to think about what might happen next or why characters behave in a particular way
- inability to relate stories or non-fiction to real life
- inability to pick out the key facts from non-fiction texts

What you can do:
- ask open-ended questions such as "Why did things happen that way?" or "What is the character doing at this point?" and "Why is this bit sad/exciting etc?" etc
- encourage children to ask themselves similar questions as they read
- encourage children to summarise or take notes

For example, in the Returning to the book section in the *Top Secret* notes, children are asked what they think the most exciting or dangerous part of the story was and give a reason for their opinion. In *Fire in the Sky*, children are asked to discuss whether Sergeant Jackson was truly brave, whether he was right or wrong to climb out onto the wing of the plane and if there was anything else he could have done. In *Long-Distance Lunch*, children are asked to discuss what they already knew and what they found surprising about where food comes from. In *Seal Skull*, children are prompted to retell the story to a partner in their own words in the past tense and using the illustrations to help them. Ask them to explain how the past tense affects the tension in the story compared with the present tense text.

Using the illustrations: visual literacy

Children today are surrounded by visual media in their daily lives in such forms as computer-generated images, advertisements, film and video, graphic novels and cartoons. Each of the texts in Progress is highly illustrated using age-appropriate images in a variety of forms and styles to appeal to different tastes, including graphic novels, manga illustrations, and stunning photography. Children are encouraged to "read" the illustrations to deepen their comprehension, interpret nuances in the texts or gain extra insight or information. Research has shown that, in particular, boys' reading and writing improves when visual literacy is specifically targeted as part of their learning.

In *In the Game*, the illustrations are vital to understanding the story as there are two stories going on at the same time. Children are asked to explore how the two storylines link or are different and find key triggers to the plot that aren't actually mentioned in the text. An example of how important visuals are in non-fiction can be seen in *Tigers in Trouble*, where children look together at a chart and describe what the information shows.

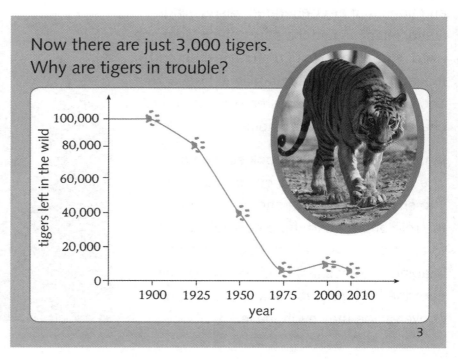

Now there are just 3,000 tigers. Why are tigers in trouble?

The last pages of each book feature a visual Reader Response activity. This provides an ideal opportunity for reflecting about the content of the text or story, and assessing children's comprehension through discussion, recalling events or emotions and relating the book to their own experiences. In *Thin Ice*, children are prompted to use the illustrations in the Reader Response activity to explain the author's viewpoint about the Antarctic. In *Winkie's War*, children are invited to retell Winkie's journey to a partner using the illustrations as a prompt, making notes of the key points.

Speaking and listening

Research has demonstrated the important role that oral language plays in the process of learning to read and write. Embedded in the teaching notes are opportunities for teachers and children to enrich understanding of the texts by questioning, explaining ideas and emotions that are generated, discussing author intention and the effect of the language used, all with a level of maturity expected by their age. Drama and role-play activities are encouraged to help children empathise with characters and explore themes.

In the Returning to the book section of *The Dolphin King* notes children are put into small groups, with one child taking the role of Jean and the others taking the roles of the other sailors. They're asked to imagine Jean has just returned to the ship from the bottom of the sea and enact the conversation they might have.

Checking and moving on

Stimulating activities for extending children's reading experience and moving into the wider curriculum include drama activities, writing, painting or modelling and further research. Two or three activities are suggested in the final section of the notes to take the children's experience beyond the pages of the book.

For example, in the Checking and moving on section in the *World's Most Deadly Creatures* notes the children are set the task of researching another deadly animal that isn't in the book, using texts or the internet. They're also given papier mâché or other modelling material and asked to make a model of a different deadly creature. In *The Deadly Monster*, children are invited to research the story of Perseus and Medusa and present it in the form of a graphic novel.

These activities can be explored to a degree of depth that suits the time allowed, inclination of the children, ability of the group or wider learning.

Getting the most out of the notes

Use the notes as a starting point for helping children to get the best out of the books. The ideas are there as tips or guidance, not to be followed slavishly, but can be added to, omitted or extended.

They help to build up a reading experience beyond the book, making it more relevant, meaningful and enjoyable, and providing a stimulus to revisit and re-read the book which will support fluency and develop confidence.

4 Using APP to assess with confidence

The purpose of assessment is to find evidence that demonstrates where a child is in his or her learning, where they need to go next to make progress, and how they should get there.

Assessing Pupils' Progress is a structured approach that enables teachers to track children's progress in reading and writing using diagnostic information about their strengths and weaknesses.

This information is gained through:

- day-to-day observation, e.g. when pupils read both individually and within group sessions
- periodic assessment, e.g. whenever children reach a suitable point, such as the end of half-term, this can be in groups or individually, informal observation or with individual children using miscue analysis with Running Records
- transitional assessment, e.g. when children transfer to another level or year group.

No single assessment task will show that a child is at a low, secure or high level. However, observation of children over a period of time, during different occasions and using a variety of different reading material will provide evidence that they are working at a particular level for reading, and how secure they are within that level. The approach designed in APP can help teachers in that observation by providing a checklist of foci for assessment and typical child responses for each level.

APP Matching Charts, Assessment Examples and Running Records (miscue analysis)

Matching charts

Assessment Focus Matching Charts are provided on pages 48–59 to help you match the right book with the right child by choosing the criteria that will facilitate the child's learning. You can choose by topic or story subject that is of interest, desired learning objectives, reading level or interest level. The charts are organised by readability and detail the interest level, text types, curriculum links and objectives and also inform you of the appropriate assessment foci, Reading Recovery level and National Curriculum level.

Assessment examples

Assessment examples for each title are provided on pages 60–83 to help you gauge the level at which your pupils are performing. These show you sample responses of what children can do at a higher and at a lower level for both decoding at National Curriculum level 1 and language comprehension at National Curriculum levels 3–4. The lower level takes account of the child's below-age-related decoding skills, while the higher level in language comprehension is in recognition that they're likely to have better accessibility to the high-interest level subject matter due to their age and experience.

The assessment examples refer directly back to the specific teaching points contained in the teaching notes at the back of the books, and are signposted by section. For example, in *The Dolphin King*, the first assessment example is GS2 (the second bullet point in the Getting Started section): can children relate this story to other stories within this genre? This gives you a clear reference point for making day-to-day observations using the notes in an unobtrusive way as children are reading, as well as providing specific points for periodic assessment and transitional assessment.

These examples are a guide only and cannot cover all the different ways children will respond to a reading task, but they provide a useful benchmark for understanding and recognising when children are secure in their reading skills and when they are less secure.

Running Records and miscue analysis

Running Record sheets are provided for each title on pages 84–95. They can be used periodically to support APP, specifically AF1: use a range of strategies, including accurate decoding of text, to read for meaning. Wherever possible, Running Records should be conducted using previously unseen material. Ask the child to sit next to you and explain that you want to see how well they read a text aloud without any prompting. Introduce the book by looking at the front cover and title together, and then ask the child to begin reading. As he or she reads, mark the errors they make using miscue analysis symbols included on the Running Record sheets and make a note of the strategies the child uses, i.e. ph – phonic, g – graphic, s – syntactic, c – context.

Analysing the result

A 98%+ reading accuracy indicates that the book is at a comfortable level for the child's independent reading. Books at this level of accuracy can readily be sent home for reading. A 95% level of accuracy indicates that the book is at an instructional level, i.e. can be read in a guided group with support in order to improve accuracy. Below 95% indicates that the books are at too high a level, leading to frustration and suggesting that the child would benefit from reading books at a lower band

The notes made during the Running Record should give a clear picture of which strategies a pupil uses and which strategies need further practise. This helps to inform your knowledge of where a child needs further practice. For example, a child with a reading accuracy of 95% may benefit from further practice in using particular strategies before he or she moves to a higher readability band. Similarly, one child with a reading accuracy of just below 94% may benefit by reading more books in the same readability band rather than moving to a lower readability band, while another may benefit by moving to a lower readability band in order to improve reading fluency and confidence.

However, it's not just children's decoding that you're assessing. Using the Assessment Example charts can inform you about children's comprehension levels and, combined with the results of Running Records, can present an overall picture of reading fluency and which particular skills need addressing or further practice in order to make progress. For instance, if, when reading *The Dolphin King* (Blue/Copper), a child scores 95% using the Running Record, you will know this is an ideal band for guided reading, but if their responses to the comprehension aspects of the teaching notes indicate that their understanding of the story is mainly at the less-secure level, they may benefit from moving to a lower band in order to read confidently without worrying about decoding and so be able to concentrate on aspects of comprehension that need practice, such as inference and deduction.

It is important to note that a Running Record is just one type of assessment and should be used in conjunction with other assessments. The variety of questions in the teaching notes, specifically in the Returning to the text section, can help you build up a more comprehensive picture of how well children can read for meaning and will help you to gather evidence for:

- AF2 – understand and retrieve information or ideas from texts and use quotation and reference to texts
- AF3 – deduce, infer or interpret information, events or ideas from texts
- AF4 – identify and comment on the structure and organisation of texts, including grammatical and presentational features at text level
- AF5 – explain and comment on writers' use of language, including grammatical and literary features at word and sentence level
- AF6 – identify and comment on writers' purposes and viewpoints, and the overall effect of the text on the reader
- AF7 – relate texts to their social, cultural and historical contexts and literary traditions.

Your own professional judgement is invaluable in determining a child's next steps. The teaching notes inside the books, together with the APP support provided here, just act to support that judgement. They help provide evidence and enable a confident assessment of where readers are now and how to plan the approaches needed to help them move onwards and make better progress towards becoming fluent confident readers.

Assessment Focus Matching Chart

Yellow/Band 3

Title	Interest level	Text type	Curriculum links	Learning objectives (reading objectives correspond with Yellow band; all other objectives correspond with the Interest level band)	Assessment focuses	Reading recovery level	NC level
Fiction							
Mission Mars Anne Curtis	Copper/Band 12	A science-fiction story	Science: Light and shadows	• Use phonics to read unknown or difficult words	R1	4/5	Working within level 1
				• Empathise with characters and debate moral dilemmas portrayed in texts	R3		
				• Present events and characters through dialogue to engage the interest of an audience	SL1		
				• Use layout, format, graphics, illustrations for different purposes	W3		
In the Game Katy Coope	Ruby/Band 14	A graphic novel	ICT: Exploring simulations	• Read longer words including simple two- and three-syllable words	R1	4/5	Working within level 1
				• Use phonics to read unknown or difficult words	R1		
				• Deduce characters' reasons for behaviour from their actions and	R3		

Yellow/Band 3

Title	Interest level	Text type	Curriculum links	Learning objectives (reading objectives correspond with Yellow band; all other objectives correspond with the Interest level band)	Assessment focuses	Reading recovery level	NC level
Fiction							
				explain how ideas are developed in non-fiction texts	R2/R3		
				• Interrogate texts to deepen and clarify understanding and response	SL3		
				• Create roles showing how behaviour can be interpreted from different viewpoints			
				• Use settings and characterisation to engage readers' interest	W2		
Top Secret Mick Manning and Brita Granström	Sapphire/Band 16	A graphic novel set in the past	History: What can we learn about recent history by studying the life of a famous person?	• Use knowledge of words and spelling patterns to read unknown words	R1	6/7/8	Working within level 1
				• Explore how writers use language for comic and dramatic effects	R5		
				• Explore the usefulness of techniques such as visualisation in exploring the meaning of texts	R3		
				• Reflect on how working in role helps to explore complex issues	SL3		
Thin Ice Anne Curtis	Diamond/Band 17	An adventure book	History: What can we learn about recent history by studying the life of a famous person?; Geography: Weather around the world	• Use phonics to read unknown words	R1	6/7/8	Working within level 1
				• Understand underlying themes, causes and points of view	R3		
				• Recognise rhetorical devices used to argue, persuade, mislead and sway the reader	R5		
				• Use a range of oral techniques to present persuasive arguments	SL1		
				• Select words and language drawing on their knowledge of literary features and formal writing	W7		

Yellow/Band 3

Title	Interest level	Text type	Curriculum links	Learning objectives (reading objectives correspond with Yellow band; all other objectives correspond with the Interest level band)	Assessment focuses	Reading recovery level	NC level
Non-Fiction							
Cool Cars John Foster	Copper/Band 12	A non-fiction book	Design and Technology: Vehicles; Science: Forces and movement	• Use phonics to read unknown or difficult words, including the full range of digraphs to decode unknown words	R1	6/7/8	Working within level 1
				• Identify and make notes of the main points of sections of text	R2		
				• Follow up on others' points to show whether they agree or disagree	SL2/R3		
				• Use layout, format, graphics, illustrations for different purposes	W3		
Olympic BMX Charlotte Guillain	Ruby/Band 14	A non-fiction report	PE: Outdoor and adventurous activities	• Read longer words including simple two- and three-syllable words	R1	6/7/8	Working within level 1
				• Use phonics to read unknown or difficult words	R1		
				• Use knowledge of different organisational features of texts to find information effectively	R4		
				• Identify and summarise evidence from a text to support a hypothesis	R2/R3		
				• Interrogate texts to deepen and clarify understanding and response	R2/R3		
				• Choose and combine words, images and other features for particular effects	W4/W5/W7		
Muscles Anna Claybourne	Sapphire/Band 16	An information book	Science: Keeping healthy	• Read longer words including simple two- and three-syllable words	R1	6/7/8	Working within level 1
				• Use phonics to read unknown or difficult words	R1		
				• Make notes on and use evidence from across a text to explain events or ideas	R2		

Yellow/Band 3

Title	Interest level	Text type	Curriculum links	Learning objectives *(reading objectives correspond with Yellow band; all other objectives correspond with the Interest level band)*	Assessment focuses	Reading recovery level	NC level
Non-Fiction							
				• Adapt non-narrative forms and styles to write factual texts	W2		
When Rosa Parks Met Martin Luther King, Junior Zoë Clarke	Diamond/Band 17	A non-fiction recount	Citizenship: Living in a diverse world; History: What can we learn about recent history by studying the life of a famous person?	• Use phonics to read unknown or difficult words	R1	6/7/8	Working within level 1
				• Understand underlying themes, causes and points of view	R2/3		
				• Understand how writers use different structures to create coherence	R4		
				• Use the techniques of dialogic talk to explore ideas, topics or issues	SL2		
				• Improvise using a range of drama strategies and conventions to explore themes such as hopes, fears, desires	SL3		
				• Select words and language drawing on their knowledge of literary features and formal and informal writing	W7		

Collins Big Cat Progress

Assessment Focus Matching Chart

Blue/Band 4

Title	Interest level	Text type	Curriculum links	Learning objectives *(reading objectives correspond with Blue band; all other objectives correspond with the Interest level band)*	Assessment focuses	Reading recovery level	NC level
Fiction							
The Dolphin King Saviour Pirotta	Copper/Band 12	A story from another culture	Citizenship: Animals and us	• Use phonics to read unknown or difficult words	R1	9/10/11	Working within level 1
				• Infer characters' feelings in fiction	R2/R3		
				• Empathise with characters and debate moral dilemmas portrayed in texts	SL2		
				• Choose and prepare stories for performance, identifying appropriate expression, tone, volume and use of voices and other sounds	SL3		
				• Select and use a range of technical and descriptive vocabulary	W7		
				• Use beginning, middle and end to write narratives in which events are sequenced logically and conflicts resolved	W3		

Blue/Band 4

Title	Interest level	Text type	Curriculum links	Learning objectives (reading objectives correspond with Blue band; all other objectives correspond with the Interest level band)	Assessment focuses	Reading recovery level	NC level
Fiction							
Dinner with a Pirate Saviour Pirotta	Ruby/Band 14	A story from another culture	Citizenship: Choices	• Read longer words including simple two- and three-syllable words	R1	9/10/11	Working within level 1
				• Use phonics to read unknown or difficult words	R1		
				• Deduce characters' reasons for behaviour from their actions	R3		
				• Interrogate texts to deepen and clarify understanding and response	R2/R3		
				• Develop and refine ideas in writing using planning	W2		
Seal Skull Anne Curtis	Sapphire/Band 16	A mystery story	Citizenship: Animals and us	• Use phonics to read unknown or difficult words	R1	9/10/11	Working within level 1
				• Explore how writers use language for dramatic effects	R5		
				• Compare the usefulness of techniques such as visualisation in exploring the meaning of texts	R3		
				• Experiment with different narrative forms and styles to write their own stories	W2		
Fire in the Sky! Mick Manning and Brita Granström	Diamond/Band 17	A graphic novel set in the past	History: What are we remembering on Remembrance Day?	• Use phonics to read unknown words; understand underlying themes, causes and points of view	R1	9/10/11	Working within level 1
				• Use the technique of dialogic talk to explore ideas, topics or issues	SL2		
				• Select words and language drawing on their knowledge of literary features and formal and informal writing	W7		

Blue/Band 4

Title	Interest level	Text type	Curriculum links	Learning objectives (reading objectives correspond with Blue band; all other objectives correspond with the Interest level band)	Assessment focuses	Reading recovery level	NC level
Non-Fiction							
Tigers in Trouble Louise Spilsbury	Copper/Band 12	A non-fiction book	Citizenship: Animals and us	• Use phonics to read unknown or difficult words	R1	9/10/11	Working within level 1
				• Identify and make notes of the main points of sections of text	R2		
				• Identify how different texts are organised	R4		
				• Identify features that writers use to provoke readers' reactions	R6		
				• Sustain conversation, explaining or giving reasons for their views or choices	SL1		
				• Use layout, format, graphics, illustrations for different purposes	W2		
World's Deadliest Creatures Anna Claybourne	Ruby/Band 14	An information book	Citizenship: Animals and us; Geography: Habitats	• Read longer words including simple two- and three-syllable words	R1	9/10/11	Working within level 1
				• Use phonics to read unknown or difficult words	R1		
				• Identify and summarise evidence from a text to support a hypothesis	R2		
				• Use knowledge of different organisational features of texts to find information effectively	R4		
				• Interrogate texts to deepen and clarify understanding and response	R2/R3		
				• Summarise and shape material and ideas from different sources to write convincing and informative non-narrative texts	W2		

Blue/Band 4

Title	Interest level	Text type	Curriculum links	Learning objectives (reading objectives correspond with Blue band; all other objectives correspond with the Interest level band)	Assessment focuses	Reading recovery level	NC level
Non-Fiction							
The Modern Pentathlon Zoë Clarke	Sapphire/Band 16	An information book	Citizenship: Taking part; PE: Athletic activities	• Read longer words including simple two- and three-syllable words	R1	9/10/11	Working within level 1
				• Use phonics to read unknown or difficult words	R1		
				• Compare different types of narrative and information texts and identify how they are structured	R4/R7		
				• Use evidence from across a text to explain events or ideas	R2/R3		
Animals in War Jillian Powell and Imperial War Museums	Diamond/Band 17	A non-chronological report	History: What was it like to live here in the past?; Citizenship: Animals and us	• Use phonics to read unknown words	R1	9/10/11	Working within level 1
				• Understand underlying themes, causes and points of view	R2		
				• Appraise a text quickly, deciding on its value, quality or usefulness	R2/R6		
				• Use the techniques of dialogic talk to explore ideas, topics or issues	SL2		
				• Use varied structures to shape and organise text coherently	W3		

Collins Big Cat Progress

Assessment Focus Matching Chart

Green/Band 5

Title	Interest level	Text type	Curriculum links	Learning objectives (reading objectives correspond with Green band; all other objectives correspond with the Interest level band)	Assessment focuses	Reading recovery level	NC level
Fiction							
The Deadly Monster Linda Chapman	Copper/Band 12	A graphic novel	History: Who were the Ancient Greeks?	• Use phonics to read unknown or difficult words	R1	12/13/14	Working within level 1
				• Infer characters' feelings in fiction	R3		
				• Empathise with characters and debate moral dilemmas portrayed in texts	R3/SL2		
				• Use layout, format, graphics, illustrations for different purposes	W3		
Zara and the Fairy Godbrother Margaret Ryan	Ruby/Band 14	A fantasy story	ICT: Writing for different audiences	• Read longer words including simple two- and three-syllable words	R1	12/13/14	Working within level 1
				• Use phonics to read unknown or difficult words	R1		
				• Recognise all common digraphs and trigraphs, including more complex long vowel phonemes	R1		
				• Use syntax and context to self-correct when reading for accuracy and meaning	R1		

Green/Band 5

Title	Interest level	Text type	Curriculum links	Learning objectives (reading objectives correspond with Green band; all other objectives correspond with the Interest level band)	Assessment focuses	Reading recovery level	NC level
Fiction							
				• Tell stories effectively and convey detailed information coherently for listeners	SL1		
				• Interrogate texts to deepen and clarify understanding and response	R2/R3/W7		
				• Show imagination through language used to create emphasis, humour, atmosphere or suspense	W1/W7		
Winkie's War Mick Manning and Brita Granström	Sapphire/Band 16	A graphic novel set in the past	Citizenship: Animals and us	• Use phonics to read unknown words	R1	12/13/14	Working within level 1
				• Make notes on and use evidence from across a text to explain events or ideas	R2		
				• Explore how writers use language for dramatic effects	R5		
				• Present a spoken argument, sequencing points logically, defending views with evidence and making use of persuasive language	SL1		
				• Integrate words, images and sounds imaginatively for different purposes	W2		
Angel House Ann Curtis	Diamond/Band 17	A fantasy story	Citizenship: Taking part; Citizenship: Choices	• Use phonics to read unknown or difficult words	R1	12/13/14	Working within level 1
				• Appraise a text quickly, deciding on its value/quality/usefulness	R2		
				• Understand underlying themes, causes and points of view	R2/R3		
				• Use the techniques of dialogic talk to explore ideas, topics or issues	SL2		
				• Integrate words, images and sounds imaginatively for different purposes	W2		

Green/Band 5

Title	Interest level	Text type	Curriculum links	Learning objectives (reading objectives correspond with Green band; all other objectives correspond with the Interest level band)	Assessment focuses	Reading recovery level	NC level
Non-Fiction							
Natural Disasters Adrian Bradbury	Copper/Band 12	An information book	Geography: Weather around the world	• Use phonics to read unknown or difficult words	R1	12/13/14	Working within level 1
				• Use syntax and context to self-correct when reading for accuracy and meaning	R1		
				• Identify how different texts are organised	R4/R7		
				• Write non-narrative texts using structures of different text-types	W2/W3		
Long-Distance Lunch Anita Ganeri	Ruby/Band 14	A non-fiction report	Geography: Connecting ourselves to the world; Citizenship: Living in a diverse world	• Use phonics to read unknown or difficult words	R1	12/13/14	Working within level 1
				• Use knowledge of word structure and a more extensive range of prefixes and suffixes to construct the meaning of words in context	R1		
				• Use knowledge of different organisational features of texts to find information effectively	R4		
				• Interrogate texts to deepen and clarify understanding and response	R2		
				• Summarise and shape material and ideas from different sources to write convincing and informative non-narrative texts	W2		
Amazing Escapes John Foster	Sapphire/Band 16	A non-fiction recount	Citizenship: People who help us	• Use phonics to read unknown or difficult words	R1	12/13/14	Working within level 1
				• Reflect on how working in role helps to explore complex issues	SL3		

Green/Band 5

Title	Interest level	Text type	Curriculum links	Learning objectives *(reading objectives correspond with Green band; all other objectives correspond with the Interest level band)*	Assessment focuses	Reading recovery level	NC level
Non-Fiction							
				• Use knowledge of words, roots, derivations and spelling patterns to read unknown words	R1		
				• Use evidence from across a text to explain events or ideas	R2		
				• Reflect independently and critically on own writing and edit and improve it	W2		
Growing up in Wartime Jillian Powell and Imperial War Museums	Diamond/Band 17	A non-chronological report	History: What was it like for children in the Second World War?	• Use phonics to read unknown words • Appraise a text quickly, deciding on its value/quality/usefulness	R1 R2	12/13/14	Working within level 1
				• Understand underlying themes, causes and points of view	R2/R3		
				• Improvise using a range of drama strategies and conventions to explore themes such as hopes, fears, desires	SL3		

Assessment Examples

Key:

Ideas for Guided Reading Bullet:
GS = Getting started;
RR = Reading and responding;
RTB = Returning to the book;
CMO = Checking and moving on

APP Assessment Focus:
R = Reading;
SL= Speaking and Listening;
W = Writing

Yellow/Band 3

Title and author	Interest level	Bullet GS RR RTB	Assessment can children:	Example response (higher) Decoding: NC level 1 Language comprehension: Working towards level 3	Example response (lower) Decoding: Working towards level 1 Language comprehension: NC level 2	Assessment focuses
Fiction						
Mission Mars Anne Curtis	Copper/Band 12	GS1	recognise the genre of this story	Children can identify that this is a science-fiction story	Children are not aware of different fiction genres	R7
		RR1	decode familiar and unfamiliar words using phonic strategies, e.g. blending as a prime approach	Children can read the unfamiliar word *Orca* by blending sounds; children attempt familiar words, e.g. *f-ai-l-ed*, using phonic knowledge and familiarity with word endings	Children need support to blend sounds and apply word knowledge	R1
		RR4	interpret information from the story	Children can explain who is speaking in the speech bubbles on pp.3–4, e.g. *the voices are from inside the spaceship*	Children need help to make interpretations about who is speaking	R3
		RTB1	retrieve information from the story and retell it	Children can use the pictures on pp.14–15 to retell the story accurately to a partner, making reference to the events	Children retell parts of the story to a partner	R2/SL1

Yellow/Band 3

Title and author	Interest level	Bullet GS RR RTB	Assessment can children:	Example response (higher) Decoding: NC level 1 Language comprehension: Working towards level 3	Example response (lower) Decoding: Working towards level 1 Language comprehension: NC level 2	Assessment focuses
Non-fiction						
Cool Cars John Foster	Copper/Band 12	GS2	interpret the information in the blurb and discuss their ideas about the cars described	Children can describe how a parachute is used to slow down a really fast car, e.g. *it shoots out of the back*	Children need encouragement to suggest ideas about how a parachute can be used	R3/SL1
		GS3	decode familiar and unfamiliar words using phonic strategies, e.g. blending as a prime approach	Children can read the contents, blending phonemes in longer words e.g. *f-l-y-i-ng*, *f-l-oa-t-i-ng*. Children use phonic knowledge and knowledge of word endings to attempt unfamiliar words, e.g. *features*, *racing*	Children need support to blend sounds and to recognise familiar word endings, e.g. *ing*	R1
		GS4	retrieve information and make notes from their reading	Children can read a chapter and make notes of key information, e.g. *some cars have wings* p.10	Children can respond to questions to support their note-making	R2
		RTB3	deduce and present information based on their reading	Using the information on pp.14–15, children can choose the most unusual car and give their reasons for this, based on deduction, e.g. *the Mercedes SL600 is the most unusual because it is covered in expensive jewellery and must be very valuable*	Children need prompting to make deductions based on their reading	R3/SL1

Yellow/Band 3

Title and author	Interest level	Bullet GS RR RTB	Assessment can children:	Example response (higher) Decoding: NC level 1 Language comprehension: NC level 3	Example response (lower) Decoding: Working towards level 1 Language comprehension: Working towards level 3	Assessment focuses
Fiction						
In the Game Katy Coope	Ruby/Band 14	GS2	identify the features that they expect to see in a graphic novel	Children can describe the features that will carry the story, e.g. *cartoon strip pictures, manga images, speech bubbles*, and relate these to other graphic texts they have experienced	Children know that this is a cartoon-style story	R7
		RR1	use phonic knowledge and strategies to read familiar words	Children can recognise the *y* suffix in *hungry* and blend the phonemes in the word to read *h-u-n-g-r-y*	Children need help to identify the *y* suffix and blend through the word *h-u-n-g-r-y*	R1
		RR2	decode familiar and unfamiliar words using blending as a prime approach	Children use knowledge of syllables alongside phonic knowledge to read longer words, e.g. *happ-en-ing*	Children need support to attempt longer words using blending as a prime approach	R1
		RTB2	compare the two storylines and demonstrate that they understand the plot by describing their ideas	Children use the images on pp.14–15 to describe the two storylines and how they link. Children may infer that the alien invasion is connected to the game play, e.g. *the alien explodes when the children win the game*	Children identify what the aliens want to do, but do not link the two story lines	R3/SL1

Yellow/Band 3

Title and author	Interest level	Bullet GS RR RTB	Assessment can children:	Example response (higher) Decoding: NC level 1 Language comprehension: NC level 3	Example response (lower) Decoding: Working towards level 1 Language comprehension: Working towards level 3	Assessment focuses
Non-fiction						
Olympic BMX Charlotte Guillain	Ruby/Band 14	GS3	interpret the information in the blurb and discuss what sort of book this is	Children can identify that this is a non-fiction book and can recognise and discuss other features of non-fiction books and their usefulness, e.g. *photos, labels etc*	Children need support to recognise the features of a non-fiction book and their purpose	R7/SL1
		RR1	read independently using a variety of cues to make meaning	Children can read the text on their own using a range of strategies to decode unfamiliar words, e.g. *helmet, gloves p.11*	Children over-rely on one key strategy and need help to use the full range of strategies to make meaning	R1
		RR2	interpret information from the text	Children look closely at the photos on pp.4–5 and make comparisons between the two bikes, e.g. *BMX bikes have thicker tyres to go on rough ground*	Children need help to find information in the photos and make comparisons between the bikes	R3
		RTB1	retrieve information from the text	Children look closely at the pp.14–15 and discuss the sorts of training featured, e.g. *you need to practise jumping and keep fit*	Children need help to understand the kind of training required to race BMX bikes	R2/SL1

Yellow/Band 3

Title and author	Interest level	Bullet GS RR RTB	Assessment can children:	Example response (higher) Decoding: Working towards level 2 Language comprehension: Working towards level 4	Example response (lower) Decoding: NC level 1 Language comprehension: NC level 3	Assessment focuses
Fiction						
Top Secret Mick Manning and Brita Granström	Sapphire/Band 16	GS2	interpret information from the blurb	Children decide whether this is a true story from looking at the back cover, reading the blurb and own knowledge	Children answer questions about the back cover and the blurb	R2/SL1
		RR2	decode familiar and unfamiliar words using phonic strategies, e.g. blending and other strategies	Children can read the unfamiliar words *secret agent* p.2, *officer* p.12 etc using phonic strategies and word knowledge	Children need support to blend sounds and apply word knowledge	R1
		RR3	interpret information from the story	Children can explain who is speaking in the speech bubbles, e.g. on p.2 *the man in the plane behind Christine is telling her to jump*	Children need help to make interpretations about who is speaking	R3
		RTB1	retrieve information from the story and retell it	Children can use the illustrations on pp.14–5 to retell the story of Christine Granville accurately to a partner, making reference to the events in her life	Children can retell parts of the story to a partner	R2/SL1/SL2

Yellow/Band 3

Title and author	Interest level	Bullet GS RR RTB	Assessment can children:	Example response (higher) Decoding: Working towards level 2 Language comprehension: Working towards level 4	Example response (lower) Decoding: NC level 1 Language comprehension: NC level 3	Assessment focuses
Non-fiction						
Muscles Anna Claybourne	Sapphire/Band 16	GS2	comment on the organisational features of this book at text level	Children can identify that this is a non-fiction book and can recognise some of the features, e.g. contents, glossary	Children need help to recognise the organisational features	R7
		RR1	decode familiar and unfamiliar words using phonic strategies and recognition of high frequency words	Children recognise high frequency words, e.g. *there* p.2 etc. Children can use phonic knowledge to work out new words, e.g. they can recognise the hard *c* sound of *ch* in *s/t/o/m/a/ch* p.3	Children need support to recognise high frequency words and use phonic strategies to read less familiar words	R1
		RR2	interpret information from the book	Children can identify their own arm muscles from the illustrations on pp.4–7	Children need help to understand the illustrations on pp.4–7 and relate them to their own arm muscles	R3
		RTB1	recall and present information based on their reading	Children can use the information on pp.14–15 to say how each type of muscle does its job, e.g. *the heart muscle pumps blood around your body*	Children need prompting to recall what they have read and use information	R2/SL1

Yellow/Band 3

Title and author	Interest level	Bullet GS RR RTB	Assessment can children:	Example response (higher) Decoding: Working towards level 2 Language comprehension: NC level 4	Example response (lower) Decoding: NC level 1 Language comprehension: Working towards level 4	Assessment focuses
Fiction						
Thin Ice Anne Curtis	Diamond/Band 17	GS1	predict information about events from the front cover	Children describe what the story will be about, e.g. *this looks like a really cold and lonely place with snow and ice*	Children answer questions about the picture on the front cover	R2
		RR1	decode familiar and unfamiliar words using phonic strategies, e.g. blending and other strategies	Children use word knowledge and phonic strategies to read interest words, e.g. *blizzard* p.4, *diaries* p.8 etc	Children need support to blend sounds and apply word knowledge	R1
		RR3	interpret information from the story	Looking at the illustrations on pp.10–11 children can explain whether this is in the present or in the past and why	Children need help to understand the illustrations and sense of time in the book	R3
		RTB1	retrieve information from the story and retell it	Children can use the information on pp.14–15 to discuss how the Antarctic has changed since Scott's time and why, and whether this is a good or bad thing	Children need support to understand the issues raised in the book	R2/3/SL1

Yellow/Band 3

Title and author	Interest level	Bullet GS RR RTB	Assessment can children:	Example response (higher) Decoding: Working towards level 2 Language comprehension: NC level 4	Example response (lower) Decoding: NC level 1 Language comprehension: Working towards level 4	Assessment focuses
Non-fiction						
When Rosa Parks Met Martin Luther King, Junior Zoë Clarke	Diamond/Band 17	GS2	explain and comment on writer's use of language	When looking at the blurb children can discuss the meaning of the phrase *fought for change* and discuss the link between this and the sort of events that will be in the book, e.g. *this is a true story about somebody who fought for the rights of black people*	Children do not understand the meaning of *fought for change* and need support to understand the language in the blurb and how this links to events in the book	R5/SL2
		RR3	read independently using a variety of cues to make meaning	Children can read the text on their own using a range of strategies to decode unfamiliar words, e.g. *different* p.2, *together* p.15	Children over-rely on one key strategy and need help to use the full range of strategies to make meaning	R1
		RR1	interpret information from the text	Looking at the photos on pp.2–3 children can explain how black and white people were treated differently	Children need support to interpret the photos and their context	R3
		RTB1	retrieve information from the events in the book and retell Rosa Parks' story	Children can use the timeline on pp.14–15 to retell the events of the book to a partner and give a personal response	Children retell parts of the book to a partner using the timeline	R6/SL1

Collins Big Cat Progress

Assessment Examples

Key:

Ideas for Guided Reading Bullet:
GS = Getting started;
RR = Reading and responding;
RTB = Returning to the book;
CMO = Checking and moving on

APP Assessment Focus:
R = Reading;
SL= Speaking and Listening;
W = Writing

Blue/Band 4

Title and author	Interest level	Bullet GS RR RTB	Assessment can children:	Example response (higher) Decoding: NC level 1 Language comprehension: Working towards level 3	Example response (lower) Decoding: Working towards level 1 Language comprehension: NC level 2	Assessment focuses
Fiction						
The Dolphin King Saviour Pirotta	Copper/Band 12	GS2	relate this story to other stories within this genre	Children know that this story is a legend, e.g. they know that legends feature magical creatures and happenings, and that the story will have a moral	Children know that legends are tales from long ago	R7
		RR1	decode unfamiliar words using phonic knowledge and strategies	Children can read the word *spear* p.3, using phonic knowledge, e.g. blending the phonemes *s-p-ea-r*	Children need support to identify the long vowel phoneme *ea* in *spear*	R1
		RR2	make straightforward inferences based on a single point in the text	Children can infer that the storm was caused by the man spearing the dolphin	Children make literal interpretations, e.g. *the storm was caused by the weather*	R3
		RTB1	retrieve information from the story, making reference to the text	Children can use the illustrations on pp.14–15 to recount the stages of the story to a partner	Children need support to recount the story in stages	R2/SL1

Blue/Band 4

Title and author	Interest level	Bullet GS RR RTB	Assessment can children:	Example response (higher) Decoding: NC level 1 Language comprehension: Working towards level 3	Example response (lower) Decoding: Working towards level 1 Language comprehension: NC level 2	Assessment focuses
Non-fiction						
Tigers in Trouble Louise Spilsbury	Copper/Band 12	GS1	predict information about the book from the front cover photograph and title	Children can discuss what the book will be about, e.g. *it will be about tigers and the dangers they face*	Children answer simple questions about the picture on the front cover	R2
		GS3	decode familiar and unfamiliar words using phonic strategies, e.g. blending and other strategies	Children can read the contents page and use phonic cues and word knowledge to decode tricky words, e.g. *habitats* p.4, *danger* p.8	Children need support to blend sounds and apply word knowledge	R1
		RR2	interpret information from the story	Children can use the graph on p.3 to discuss the drop in numbers over the years and can give their reasons	Children need help to make interpretations about the graph	R3/SL1
		RTB1	retrieve information from the story and retell it	Children can use the chart on pp.14–15 to discuss the link between the drop in tiger numbers and changes in their lives	Children need help to understand the link between elements in the chart	R2/SL1

Blue/Band 4

Title and author	Interest level	Bullet GS RR RTB	Assessment can children:	Example response (higher) Decoding: NC level 1 Language comprehension: NC level 3	Example response (lower) Decoding: Working towards level 1 Language comprehension: Working towards level 3	Assessment focuses
Fiction						
Dinner with a Pirate Saviour Pirotta	Ruby/Band 14	GS1	recognise the features of a folk tale	Children recall folk tales that they know and remember that folk tales may have a moral at the ending, e.g. *one good turn deserves another*	Children have heard of folk tales but need support to remember other examples and common features	R7
		RR1	decode familiar and unfamiliar words using blending as a prime approach	Children use knowledge of syllables alongside phonic knowledge to read longer words, e.g. *fish-er-man*	Children need support to attempt longer words using blending as a prime approach	R1
		RR2	interpret information from the story	Children can infer how the pirate feels when Pedro offers to share his food, e.g. *he ate a lot because he was starving*	Children make simple inferences about how the pirate feels, e.g. *he was grateful*	R3
		RTB4	understand and describe the events in the story	Children can retell the story to a partner using their own words and making reference to the illustrations	Children rely heavily on the book when retelling the story to a partner	R2/SL1

Blue/Band 4

Title and author	Interest level	Bullet GS RR RTB	Assessment can children:	Example response (higher) Decoding: NC level 1 Language comprehension: NC level 3	Example response (lower) Decoding: Working towards level 1 Language comprehension: Working towards level 3	Assessment focuses
Non-fiction						
World's Deadliest Creatures Anna Claybourne	Ruby/Band 14	GS2	deduce, infer or interpret information from the text	Children can explain what makes creatures deadly having read the title and looked at the front cover	Children need help to interpret the information described in the title and on the front cover	R3
		RR1/ RR2	read independently using a variety of cues to make meaning	Children use phonic and picture cues, knowledge of high frequency words and contextual information to tackle interest words, e.g. *deadly* p.4, *venomous* p.8, *tentacles* p.10 etc	Children over-rely on one key strategy and need help to use the full range of strategies to make meaning	R1
		RTB1	understand and interpret ideas from the text	Using the information on pp.14–15 children can discuss how the animals are grouped on these pages, e.g. *all the ones that bite have been put together*	Children need help to explain the grouping of the animals	R2/SL1
		RTB2	retrieve information, make notes and discuss their findings	Children can read a chapter and make notes of key information for discussion	Children can respond to questions to support their note-making	R2/SL2

Blue/Band 4

Title and author	Interest level	Bullet GS RR RTB	Assessment can children:	Example response (higher) Decoding: Working towards level 2 Language comprehension: Working towards level 4	Example response (lower) Decoding: NC level 1 Language comprehension: NC level 3	Assessment focuses
Fiction						
Seal Skull Anne Curtis	Sapphire/Band 16	GS1	recognise the genre of this story from the front cover and title	Looking at the front cover children can discuss what kind of story this will be, e.g. *this will be a scary story because of the skull*	Children can make simple comments based on the front cover, e.g. *there is a beach with a big skull*	R2/SL1
		RR1	decode familiar and unfamiliar words using phonic strategies, e.g. blending and other strategies	Children can blend phonemes and apply word knowledge to read interest words, e.g. *seal* p.2, *beach* p.3, *skull* p.3 etc	Children need support to blend sounds and apply word knowledge	R1
		RR2	comment on writer's purpose and use of language	At significant parts of the story pause and ask children how they feel about the text being in the present tense, e.g. pp.6–7 *it makes it feel that it is happening now*	Children are able to make simple comments about how the story makes them feel, e.g. *the skull in the room makes it scary*	R5/R6
		RTB1	retrieve information from the story and retell it	Looking at pp.14–15 children can discuss with a partner the power of the skull in the story, e.g. *everything that happens is caused by the skull*	Children need help to understand the importance of the skull in the story	R2/R3/SL1

Blue/Band 4

Title and author	Interest level	Bullet GS RR RTB	Assessment can children:	Example response (higher) Decoding: Working towards level 2 Language comprehension: Working towards level 4	Example response (lower) Decoding: NC level 1 Language comprehension: NC level 3	Assessment focuses
Non-fiction						
The Modern Pentathlon Zoë Clarke	Sapphire/Band 16	GS1	comment on the organisational features of this book at text level	Children can discuss the picture on the front cover and predict what the book may be about, e.g. *it's a book about sport; it's a book about fencing*	Children need prompting to predict the content of the book from the front cover	R4
		RR2	decode familiar and unfamiliar words using phonic strategies, e.g. blending and other strategies	Children can read the unfamiliar word *pentathlete* p.3 by blending sounds; children attempt more familiar words, e.g. *sp-ee-d* p.14 using phonic knowledge and familiarity with word endings	Children need support to blend sounds and apply word knowledge	R1
		RR3	retrieve information from the text	Using the information on pp.4–5 children can describe what clothes are worn in fencing and show the evidence in the book, e.g. *you wear a mask to protect your face*	Children need help to find information in the photographs	R2
		RT3	interpret information from the book	Children can use the information on pp.14–15 to explain why some of the events are grouped together, e.g. *you need speed in fencing and swimming*	Children need encouragement in using the information to make inferences	R3/SL1

Blue/Band 4

Title and author	Interest level	Bullet GS RR RTB	Assessment can children:	Example response (higher) Decoding: Working towards level 2 Language comprehension: NC level 4	Example response (lower) Decoding: NC level 1 Language comprehension: Working towards level 4	Assessment focuses
Fiction						
Fire in the Sky Mick Manning and Brita Granström	Diamond/Band 17	GS3	recognise the structural features designed to support information retrieval	Children can interpret meaning using the graphic novel features, e.g. they recognise that multiple frames have been used to organise events	Children recognise that the cartoon strip carries meaning but need help to read in the right order	R2/R4
		RR1	break longer words into syllables, use familiar letter patterns, use knowledge of prefixes and suffixes, and blend elements of longer words together to read them	Children read using syllables and suffixes e.g. *sur-viv(e)-d*; *Ger-man-y* p.2; *att-ack-ed* p.3; *c-augh-t* p.3	Children need support to read familiar suffixes e.g. *ed, y* and read longer words	R1
		RR3	recognise how speech bubbles are used to add information	Children read the speech bubbles on p.4 and describe how the speech adds information, e.g. *they tell you that the crew tried to stop him*	Children recognise the speech bubbles but without describing their effect	R5
		RTB2	make accurate inferences based on evidence from throughout the text	Using pp.14–15, children can describe the emotions felt by Jackson at different stages in the story	Children make straightforward inferences about Jackson, e.g. *he was brave*	R3

Blue/Band 4

Title and author	Interest level	Bullet GS RR RTB	Assessment can children:	Example response (higher) Decoding: Working towards level 2 Language comprehension: NC level 4	Example response (lower) Decoding: NC level 1 Language comprehension: Working towards level 4	Assessment focuses
Non-fiction						
Animals in War Jillian Powell	Diamond/Band 17	RR1	break longer words into syllables, use knowledge of prefixes and suffixes, and blend elements of longer words together to read them	Children read using syllables and suffixes, e.g. *im-por-tant* p.2, *sniff-ed* p.3, *kill-ed* p.5	Children need support to read familiar suffixes, e.g. *ed*, and read longer words	R1
		RR2	understand and retrieve information from the text	Children can note three key activities of animals used in wars, e.g. *dogs sniffed out mines*	Children need support to recall specific information about how animals helped, e.g. *there were dogs*	R2
		RTB1	make accurate inferences based on evidence from illustrations	Children can use the photographs on pp.14–15 to make inferences about how the animals helped, e.g. *dogs were used to sniff out bombs because they have a stronger sense of smell than humans*	Children can make simple inferences, e.g. *the dog is helping the man*	R3
		RTB3	interpret information and express their feelings	Children can explain to a partner in detail which animal they think had the most dangerous job in war time	Children develop their interpretation of the book by discussing ideas with a partner	SL1/R3

Collins Big Cat Progress

Assessment Examples

Key:

Ideas for Guided Reading Bullet:
GS = Getting started;
RR = Reading and responding;
RTB = Returning to the book;
CMO = Checking and moving on

APP Assessment Focus:
R = Reading;
SL= Speaking and Listening;
W = Writing

Green/Band 5

Title and author	Interest level	Bullet GS RR RTB	Assessment can children:	Example response (higher) Decoding: Working towards level 2 Language comprehension: Working towards level 3	Example response (lower) Decoding: NC level 1 Language comprehension: NC level 2	Assessment focuses
Fiction						
The Deadly Monster Linda Chapman	Copper/Band 12	RR1	take account of punctuation to read with expression	Children identify speech bubbles p.2, and read their content with appropriate expression	Children need support to adopt expressive voices when reading aloud	R1/SL1
		RR2	use appropriate strategies to decode unfamiliar words	Children use phonic knowledge and contextual cues to read the words *museum, statues,* on p.2	Children over-rely on one strategy when trying to decode unfamiliar words, and need support to make meaning	R1
		RTB1	describe information contained in the text	Children can recall the skills that the boys needed in detail, using the information contained in the *wanted poster* on pp.22–23, e.g. *the boys needed to kill a deadly monster by getting the helmet*	Children need help to recall the information from the story in detail	R2
		RTB4	make meaning based on their personal response to the story	Children can give their own opinions about Jack's actions to save Sam, as part of a group discussion	Children need support to contribute their opinion to a group discussion, instead of describing the event	R3/SL2

Green/Band 5

Title and author	Interest level	Bullet GS RR RTB	Assessment can children:	Example response (higher) Decoding: Working towards level 2 Language comprehension: Working towards level 3	Example response (lower) Decoding: NC level 1 Language comprehension: NC level 2	Assessment focuses
Non-fiction						
Natural Disasters Adrian Bradbury	Copper/Band 12	GS1	interpret the information given in the title and front cover	Children can discuss why some disasters are called natural, e.g. *a flood is a natural disaster because it is caused by nature*	Children need prompting to understand the title and information on the front cover	R3/SL1
		RR1	decode familiar and some unfamiliar words using phonic strategies, e.g. blending and other strategies	Children can recognise high frequency words in their reading, e.g. *most* p.7. Children attempt less familiar words using phonic knowledge and strategies, e.g. *harsh* p.2	Children need support to recognise high frequency words, blend sounds and apply word knowledge	R1
		RR2	interpret information from the book	Children can explain from the map on p.7 what symbols mean and where hurricanes occur	Children need help to explain information on the map on p.7	R4
		RTB1	discuss ideas based on reading to develop their understanding	Children can discuss ideas and make simple inferences based on reading pp.22–23, e.g. *all these disasters cause a lot of damage to houses and people*	Children need help to discuss ideas and see what effects all the disasters have in common	R2/SL1/SL2

Green/Band 5

Title and author	Interest level	Bullet GS RR RTB	Assessment can children:	Example response (higher) Decoding: Working towards level 2 Language comprehension: NC level 3	Example response (lower) Decoding: NC level 1 Language comprehension: Working towards level 3	Assessment focuses
Fiction						
Zara and the Fairy Godbrother Margaret Ryan Illustrator Sholto Walker	Ruby/Band 14	GS1	predict information about the characters and events from the covers and title	Children predict what kind of story this will be and give reasons, e.g. *this is going to be a funny fantasy story about a girl with a fairy godbrother*	Children need support make predictions	R2
		RR1	use phonic strategies and picture cueing to read unknown and difficult words	Children can read unfamiliar words, e.g. *pantomimes* p.7, *purple* p.9, *disguise* p.21, etc by using phonic strategies and picture cues	Children over-rely on one key strategy and need help to use the full range of strategies to make meaning	R1
		RR4	explain and comment on author's use of language	Children can recognise the play on words in *a dress* and *address* on pp.17–18	Children need help to understand the play on words	R5
		RTB1	understand, describe and retell events and ideas from the text	Children can use the illustration on pp.22–23 to role-play the story accurately to a partner, making reference to specific events in the book	Children need help to retell the story to a partner	R2/SL1/SL2

Green/Band 5

Title and author	Interest level	Bullet GS RR RTB	Assessment can children:	Example response (higher) Decoding: Working towards level 2 Language comprehension: NC level 3	Example response (lower) Decoding: NC level 1 Language comprehension: Working towards level 3	Assessment focuses
Non-fiction						
Long-Distance Lunch Anita Ganeri	Ruby/Band 14	GS3	recognise the structural features designed to support information retrieval	Children recognise the contents, index and glossary. They can use the index to find information in the text, e.g. *information about cocoa beans is on p.12*	Children can identify the index, but need support to use it to retrieve information	R2/R4
		RR1	break longer words into syllables, use knowledge of prefixes and suffixes, and blend elements of longer words together to read them	Children read using syllables and suffixes e.g. *won-der-ed, trav-ell-ed* p.2; *har-vest-ed* p.4	Children need support to read familiar suffixes, e.g. *ed*, and read longer words	R1
		RR2	interpret information as they read and describe their ideas	Children can: identify the contents of the girl's lunch box on pp.2–3; connect the contents to the illustration; use the illustration to describe where each item originates from	Children can identify the food items but need support to understand that the map relates to where each item comes from	R3/SL1
		RTB2	find information in the text	Using the information provided on pp.22–23, children can work with a partner to find each food's country of origin	Children need support to locate information in the text, by skimming, scanning and using retrieval devices	R2

Green/Band 5

Title and author	Interest level	Bullet GS RR RTB	Assessment can children:	Example response (higher) Decoding: Working towards level 2 Language comprehension: Working towards level 4	Example response (lower) Decoding: NC level 1 Language comprehension: NC level 3	Assessment focuses
Fiction						
Winkie's War Mick Manning and Brita Granstrom	Sapphire/Band 16	GS1/ GS2	predict information about characters and events from the front cover and blurb	Children can identify what kind of information they will find in this book by looking at the front cover and the blurb, e.g. *this is about a pigeon called Winkie and what it did in the war*	Children need help to predict the kind of information contained in the book	R2/SL2
		RR1	decode familiar and unfamiliar words using phonic strategies and word knowledge	Children can read unfamiliar words e.g. *travelling p.4, navigator p.5,* by using phonic strategies and word knowledge	Children need support to blend sounds and apply word knowledge	R1
		RR3	interpret information from the story	Children can explain what is happening in the story using illustrations and text, e.g. pp.8–9 *they are sending the pigeon to get help*	Children can respond to questions about the illustrations, e.g. *the plane has crashed*	R3
		RTB1	identify overall effect of the text on the reader	Children can use the information on pp.22–23 to retell the story accurately to a partner and give a personal response to the story	Children need help to retell the story to a partner and to give a personal response	R6/SL1

Green/Band 5

Title and author	Interest level	Bullet GS RR RTB	Assessment can children:	Example response (higher) Decoding: Working towards level 2 Language comprehension: Working towards level 4	Example response (lower) Decoding: NC level 1 Language comprehension: NC level 3	Assessment focuses
Non-fiction						
Amazing Escapes John Foster	Sapphire/Band 16	GS1	make accurate inferences based on evidence from the front cover	Children can infer that the people in the illustration are miners who have escaped from a mining accident, e.g. *they are wearing headtorches and must have escaped from underground*	Children make straightforward inferences, e.g. *he is happy because he has escaped*	R3
		RR2	find words within longer words to assist their decoding	Children can read longer words, e.g. *skydiver, firefighter* pp.4–5, by breaking them into smaller known words and using knowledge of the *er* suffix	Children need support to read longer words and rely on blending as a prime strategy	R1
		RR3	understand and retrieve information from the text	Children can make further meaning by referring to the illustrations and captions, e.g. p.5 *he broke his helmet when he landed on the metal roof*	Children can answer questions about additional information but need support to make meaning, e.g. *he is holding a helmet*	R2
		RTB1	speak in an extended turn to describe their reading	Using pp.22–23, and making reference to the appropriate section of the text, children describe an escape to a partner and explain what was impressive about it	Children recount an escape, but need support to elaborate their ideas and make reference to the text	SL1/R2

Green/Band 5

Title and author	Interest level	Bullet GS RR RTB	Assessment can children:	Example response (higher) Decoding: Working towards level 2 / Language comprehension: NC level 4	Example response (lower) Decoding: NC level 1 / Language comprehension: Working towards level 4	Assessment focuses
Fiction						
Angel House Ann Curtis	Diamond/Band 17	GS1	identify that this book may be a mystery story from the front and back covers	Children relate this book to other mystery or ghost stories that they have read, based on their awareness of the genre, e.g. *the illustration of a spooky house; the meaning of the title*	Children recognise that this book is a mysterious story by its front cover and the blurb	R7
		GS2	comment on the writer's use of language for effect	Children notice that the story is written in the first person (*I*). They identify that this adds to the mystery of the story because you do not know the identity of the narrator	Children understand that the story is told by a narrator, but do not comment on the effect	R5
		RR1	use appropriate strategies to decode unfamiliar words	Children sound out and blend longer words, e.g. *s-p-e-c-i-a-l*, and use word knowledge to read them correctly, e.g. pronouncing *sh* in *special* when blended	Children rely on blending and do not use word knowledge to pronounce words correctly, e.g. *special, belong*	R1
		RTB3	understand ideas from the texts and interpret information	Children can use the feeling staircase on pp.22–23 to relate each feeling and comment to a point in the story. They can describe their ideas to the group	Children need support to relate each step on the staircase to the feeling described	R2/R3/SL1

Green/Band 5

Title and author	Interest level	Bullet GS RR RTB	Assessment can children:	Example response (higher) Decoding: Working towards level 2 Language comprehension: NC level 4	Example response (lower) Decoding: NC level 1 Language comprehension: Working towards level 4	Assessment focuses
Non-fiction						
Growing up in Wartime Jillian Powell	Diamond/Band 17	GS2	decode unfamiliar words using appropriate strategies	Children can read the contents aloud using knowledge of letter strings and phonic skills to decode unfamiliar words, e.g. *en-ter-tain-ment, ra-tion*	Children rely on blending, but do not recognise common letter strings as units	R1
		RR2	describe their reading by making relevant reference to the text	Children can recount what is happening in the pictures on pp.2–3, e.g. *the little boy's home has been bombed and he is placing a flag in the rubble*	Children need help to make relevant reference to the text, e.g. *he is playing with a flag*	R2/R3
		RTB1	infer information from the text	Using the information on pp.22–23, children can infer how the children in the pictures are feeling, e.g. *food was rationed, which meant that they couldn't eat what they wanted and didn't have as much as we do*	Children make simple inferences, e.g. *she is writing a letter; she has a toy dog*	R3
		RTB4	identify the purpose of the book and evaluate the content	Children can explain to others what they have learnt from reading this book, and evaluate whether it can be recommended for other readers	Children need help to reach an opinion about the value of the book	SL1/R6

Running Record Sheet

Child's name: _____   Date: _____

Cool Cars   **Band: Yellow/Copper**

Page no.	Text	Strategies used: Phonic (ph), Graphic (g), Syntactic (s), Contextual (c)
4	**Fast Cars** These cars can go at more than 400 kilometres per hour.	
5	This car goes so fast that it has a parachute to slow it down so it can stop safely.	
6	**Racing cars and bangers** These cars race at more than 300 kilometres per hour.	
7	There are many crashes *(50 words)* when bangers race.	
Total miscues out of 50		

Accuracy table

No. of miscues out of 50	0	1	2	3	4	5	6	7	8	9	10
Accuracy rate %	100%	98%	96%	94%	92%	90%	88%	86%	84%	82%	80%

Book level matching guidance

For children reading with:

- 96%-100% accuracy (2 or less miscues): The child can read this text independently and may be ready for the next colour band for guided reading sessions.

- 90-95% accuracy (3-5 miscues): The child can read this text with guidance and instruction. This is the *ideal band* for guided reading sessions.

- Below 90% accuracy (6 or more miscues): The child may struggle to maintain an understanding of this text within a guided reading session and may be better suited to a lower band..

Running Record Procedure

- Check that the child is ready and happy to proceed.
- Provide the child with the book. Introduce the book but do not describe the content.
- Explain that you are going to listen and make notes while the child reads to you.
- Allow the child to read. Only interrupt to give a word when the child has made a good attempt to read it. Make a note of strategies used to tackle tricky words.
- After reading, ask the child to tell you about the story, or to answer some questions about the story. Include recall and inference questions.
- Praise the child and thank them.

Running Record Assessment Key	
Accurate reading behaviour	**Coding**
No reading errors	Tick the word
Child self corrects the word/words	Write SC
Miscues	
Teacher tells the child the word	Write T above the word
Child omits the word	Write O above the word
Child inserts a word	Write the word above the text
Child substitutes a word	Write the word above the text
Child rereads a word, phrase or sentence	Draw an arrow around the reread text and indicate number of attempts

Running Record Sheet

Child's name: Date:

Thin Ice   Band: Yellow/Diamond

Page no.	Text	Strategies used: Phonic (ph), Graphic (g), Syntactic (s), Contextual (c)
8	Scott's diaries were inside. I read about his journey, and what he did in the Antarctic.	
10	Scott and his crew had made notes on the animals and weather to send back home. Nothing had changed here for thousands of years.	
12	But now everything is changing. One day we might drill *(50 words)* for oil here. And everything Scott found will be lost.	
Total miscues out of 50		

Accuracy table

No. of miscues out of 50	0	1	2	3	4	5	6	7	8	9	10
Accuracy rate %	100%	98%	96%	94%	92%	90%	88%	86%	84%	82%	80%

Book level matching guidance

For children reading with:

- 96%-100% accuracy (2 or less miscues): The child can read this text independently and may be ready for the next colour band for guided reading sessions.

- 90-95% accuracy (3-5 miscues): The child can read this text with guidance and instruction. This is the *ideal band* for guided reading sessions.

- Below 90% accuracy (6 or more miscues): The child may struggle to maintain an understanding of this text within a guided reading session and may be better suited to a lower band.

Running Record Procedure

- Check that the child is ready and happy to proceed.
- Provide the child with the book. Introduce the book but do not describe the content.
- Explain that you are going to listen and make notes while the child reads to you.
- Allow the child to read. Only interrupt to give a word when the child has made a good attempt to read it. Make a note of strategies used to tackle tricky words.
- After reading, ask the child to tell you about the story, or to answer some questions about the story. Include recall and inference questions.
- Praise the child and thank them.

Running Record Assessment Key	
Accurate reading behaviour	**Coding**
No reading errors	Tick the word
Child self corrects the word/words	Write SC
Miscues	
Teacher tells the child the word	Write T above the word
Child omits the word	Write O above the word
Child inserts a word	Write the word above the text
Child substitutes a word	Write the word above the text
Child rereads a word, phrase or sentence	Draw an arrow around the reread text and indicate number of attempts

Running Record Sheet

Child's name: Date:

The Dolphin King   **Band: Blue/Copper**

Page no.	Text	Strategies used: Phonic (ph), Graphic (g), Syntactic (s), Contextual (c)
4	The animal screamed and dived beneath the waves.	
5	Suddenly, a fierce storm blew up and it looked as though the boat might sink.	
6	Then Jean and his friends saw a strange knight rising out of the waves.	
7	The knight shouted, "You nearly killed the dolphin king, and for this, you'll *(50 words)* all drown!"	
Total miscues out of 50		

Accuracy table

No. of miscues out of 50	0	1	2	3	4	5	6	7	8	9	10
Accuracy rate %	100%	98%	96%	94%	92%	90%	88%	86%	84%	82%	80%

Book level matching guidance

For children reading with:

- 96%-100% accuracy (2 or less miscues): The child can read this text independently and may be ready for the next colour band for guided reading sessions.

- 90-95% accuracy (3-5 miscues): The child can read this text with guidance and instruction. This is the *ideal band* for guided reading sessions.

- Below 90% accuracy (6 or more miscues): The child may struggle to maintain an understanding of this text within a guided reading session and may be better suited to a lower band.

Running Record Procedure

- Check that the child is ready and happy to proceed.
- Provide the child with the book. Introduce the book but do not describe the content.
- Explain that you are going to listen and make notes while the child reads to you.
- Allow the child to read. Only interrupt to give a word when the child has made a good attempt to read it. Make a note of strategies used to tackle tricky words.
- After reading, ask the child to tell you about the story, or to answer some questions about the story. Include recall and inference questions.
- Praise the child and thank them.

Running Record Assessment Key	
Accurate reading behaviour	**Coding**
No reading errors	Tick the word
Child self corrects the word/words	Write SC
Miscues	
Teacher tells the child the word	Write T above the word
Child omits the word	Write O above the word
Child inserts a word	Write the word above the text
Child substitutes a word	Write the word above the text
Child rereads a word, phrase or sentence	Draw an arrow around the reread text and indicate number of attempts

Collins
Big Cat
Progress

Running Record Sheet

Child's name: Date:

Animals in War   Band: Blue/Diamond

Page no.	Text	Strategies used: Phonic (ph), Graphic (g), Syntactic (s), Contextual (c)
6	**Elephants** Elephants pulled heavy loads too.	
7	They helped to build bridges and clear roads. They could cross rivers and get into jungles to rescue people trapped by war.	
8	**Pigeons** Pigeons carried important messages home when radio could not be used.	
9	The pigeon carried a tiny metal container on its leg. The message was rolled up inside it.	
10	**Dogs** Dogs carried messages too, in containers on their collars. They also sniffed out mines or wounded men.	
11	"Paradogs" jumped from planes with parachute troops. As soon as they landed, they used their noses and ears to warn soldiers if there was danger *(100 words)* from mines or enemy troops.	
Total miscues out of 100		

Accuracy table

No. of miscues out of 100	0	1	2	3	4	5	6	7	8	9	10
Accuracy rate %	100%	98%	96%	94%	92%	90%	88%	86%	84%	82%	80%

Book level matching guidance

For children reading with:

- 96%-100% accuracy (2 or less miscues): The child can read this text independently and may be ready for the next colour band for guided reading sessions.

- 90-95% accuracy (3-5 miscues): The child can read this text with guidance and instruction. This is the *ideal band* for guided reading sessions.

- Below 90% accuracy (6 or more miscues): The child may struggle to maintain an understanding of this text within a guided reading session and may be better suited to a lower band.

Running Record Procedure

- Check that the child is ready and happy to proceed.
- Provide the child with the book. Introduce the book but do not describe the content.
- Explain that you are going to listen and make notes while the child reads to you.
- Allow the child to read. Only interrupt to give a word when the child has made a good attempt to read it. Make a note of strategies used to tackle tricky words.
- After reading, ask the child to tell you about the story, or to answer some questions about the story. Include recall and inference questions.
- Praise the child and thank them.

Running Record Assessment Key	
Accurate reading behaviour	**Coding**
No reading errors	Tick the word
Child self corrects the word/words	Write SC
Miscues	
Teacher tells the child the word	Write T above the word
Child omits the word	Write O above the word
Child inserts a word	Write the word above the text
Child substitutes a word	Write the word above the text
Child rereads a word, phrase or sentence	Draw an arrow around the reread text and indicate number of attempts

Running Record Sheet

Child's name: Date:

The Deadly Monster   Band: Green/Copper

Page no.	Text	Strategies used: Phonic (ph), Graphic (g), Syntactic (s), Contextual (c)
6	I'm Perseus, the hero.	
7	A god has turned me into a statue. "I must be free by sunset or I'll be stone forever. One touch from my sword can free me, but I cannot get it."	
8	We'll get it! Where is it? In the caves under this temple. But a bull-serpent guards it. His spit is poisonous.	
9	My helmet will help you! The boys took the helmet and ran into the caves.	
10	Suddenly they heard a noise ...	
11	A golden sword lay behind the snoring monster.	
12	How will we get to it? I'll sneak up!	
13	Jack held his breath. Could Sam get the *(100 words)* sword?	
Total miscues out of 100		

Accuracy table

No. of miscues out of 100	0	1	2	3	4	5	6	7	8	9	10
Accuracy rate %	100%	98%	96%	94%	92%	90%	88%	86%	84%	82%	80%

Book level matching guidance

For children reading with:

- 96%-100% accuracy (2 or less miscues): The child can read this text independently and may be ready for the next colour band for guided reading sessions.

- 90-95% accuracy (3-5 miscues): The child can read this text with guidance and instruction. This is the *ideal band* for guided reading sessions.

- Below 90% accuracy (6 or more miscues): The child may struggle to maintain an understanding of this text within a guided reading session and may be better suited to a lower band.

Running Record Procedure

- Check that the child is ready and happy to proceed.
- Provide the child with the book. Introduce the book but do not describe the content.
- Explain that you are going to listen and make notes while the child reads to you.
- Allow the child to read. Only interrupt to give a word when the child has made a good attempt to read it. Make a note of strategies used to tackle tricky words.
- After reading, ask the child to tell you about the story, or to answer some questions about the story. Include recall and inference questions.
- Praise the child and thank them.

Running Record Assessment Key

Accurate reading behaviour	Coding
No reading errors	Tick the word
Child self corrects the word/words	Write SC
Miscues	
Teacher tells the child the word	Write T above the word
Child omits the word	Write O above the word
Child inserts a word	Write the word above the text
Child substitutes a word	Write the word above the text
Child rereads a word, phrase or sentence	Draw an arrow around the reread text and indicate number of attempts

Running Record Sheet

Child's name: Date:

Angel House   **Band: Green/Diamond**

Page no.	Text	Strategies used: Phonic (ph), Graphic (g), Syntactic (s), Contextual (c)
6	There's an old house near where I live. The house has big metal gates.	
7	On the gates are the words *Angel House.*	
8	No one lives at Angel House. It's empty. Angel House is like a huge, dark flower in a wild garden.	
9	The path is covered with grass. The grass reaches past my waist.	
10	There are angels carved above the door. More angels are painted on the glass windows.	
11	When I step inside, the house is still and quiet. When I step inside, I feel different.	
12	I walk from room to room and as I walk feathers appear.	
13	Hundreds of *(100 words)* small, white feathers.	
Total miscues out of 100		

Accuracy table

No. of miscues out of 100	0	1	2	3	4	5	6	7	8	9	10
Accuracy rate %	100%	98%	96%	94%	92%	90%	88%	86%	84%	82%	80%

Book level matching guidance

For children reading with:

- 96%-100% accuracy (2 or less miscues): The child can read this text independently and may be ready for the next colour band for guided reading sessions.

- 90-95% accuracy (3-5 miscues): The child can read this text with guidance and instruction. This is the *ideal band* for guided reading sessions.

- Below 90% accuracy (6 or more miscues): The child may struggle to maintain an understanding of this text within a guided reading session and may be better suited to a lower band.

Running Record Procedure

- Check that the child is ready and happy to proceed.
- Provide the child with the book. Introduce the book but do not describe the content.
- Explain that you are going to listen and make notes while the child reads to you.
- Allow the child to read. Only interrupt to give a word when the child has made a good attempt to read it. Make a note of strategies used to tackle tricky words.
- After reading, ask the child to tell you about the story, or to answer some questions about the story. Include recall and inference questions.
- Praise the child and thank them.

Running Record Assessment Key

Accurate reading behaviour	Coding
No reading errors	Tick the word
Child self corrects the word/words	Write SC
Miscues	
Teacher tells the child the word	Write T above the word
Child omits the word	Write O above the word
Child inserts a word	Write the word above the text
Child substitutes a word	Write the word above the text
Child rereads a word, phrase or sentence	Draw an arrow around the reread text and indicate number of attempts

5 Integrating Collins Big Cat Progress with whole-class work

Due to the high interest level, stimulating visuals and exciting themes in the Collins Big Cat Progress titles, the books lend themselves to activities with able readers as well as struggling readers.

This has an added benefit for struggling readers in that they feel included, that they are not being given less interesting or valuable reading material compared to the rest of the class, which helps boost their self-esteem. It keeps them feeling integrated with their peers and gives their reading a relevance that makes it feel meaningful.

The nature of the Collins Big Cat Progress books makes them perfect for studying as part of a wider project. The fact that the texts are short and succinct but whole and complete makes them a good starter exercise or focal point – they can be read relatively quickly to engage or inspire and to help make a connection with a topic. As the books aren't being used for reading skills development in this context, the class can work together regardless of their reading ability. Working in mixed ability groups or partnerships may well be particularly beneficial to the struggling readers in terms of how they access and interpret the resources. While they won't be wrong if they interpret a text on a more superficial level, more able pupils may help them discover some of the nuances and subtleties of the texts.

On the whole though, struggling and able readers alike should be able to use the texts to explore the wider topics in equal measure, with all the children able to contribute with different interpretations, opinions, ideas and approaches to make for stimulating and exciting class work.

The Topics

Science

- *Muscles* could support Biology topics

Literacy

Lots of the fiction books could also be used as examples of specific writing styles and analysed for creative writing activities:
- *Seal Skull*: Creating an air of atmosphere and mystery in writing
- *In the Game*: Creating graphic novels; Manga books
- *Zara and the Fairy Godbrother*: Fairytales

History

There are a number of history titles that concentrate on the Second World War and provide a personal or alternative angle for whole-class topic work on that theme, for example:
- *Fire in the Sky* and *Top Secret*: Roles individuals played in the war; Acts of heroism during war time; The nature of bravery; When can doing something brave actually be foolish or endanger other people?
- *Growing up in Wartime*: What was life like for children during the war? What is life like now for children in war zones?
- *Animals in War* and *Winkie's War*: What part did animals play in World War Two? What part do or should animals play in modern wars? The nature of bravery

Other books look at different periods and areas of learning:
- *The Deadly Monster*: Ancient Greece
- *When Rosa Parks met Martin Luther King, Junior*: Black History Month

Geography

- *Long-Distance Lunch*: Food miles; Climate change and ways to make a difference
- *Cool Cars*: Transport
- *Thin Ice*: Climate change; The world's resources – how and why we use them and what the alternatives are
- *World's Deadliest Creatures* and *Tigers in Trouble*: Wildlife, including endangered species; Habitats around the world
- *Natural Disasters*: What can be done to mitigate the harmful effects of nature?
- *Mission Mars*: Space travel; Life on other planets; Could humans survive on another planet?

PSHE

The titles cover a wide range of topics within PSHE from healthy living to bullying, for example:
- *Olympic BMX* and *Modern Pentathlon*: Fitness and keeping healthy; The Olympic Games
- *Amazing Escapes*: The impact people have on each other's lives
- *Dinner with a Pirate*: Kindness and selflessness; Should good deeds be rewarded?
- *The Dolphin King* and *Seal Skull*: Causes and consequences – how what we do affects others
- *Angel House*: Bullying

The expanded examples on the following pages demonstrate, with four of the titles, how they could be used to provide a stimulus and textual reference point for a class topic.

Angel House (PSHE)

Topic: Bullying

Angel House deals with the sensitive issues of bullying, self-esteem and feeling apart or different from one's peers. With a minimal amount of text and stark illustrations, children of all reading abilities have a great opportunity to practise skills of inference and deduction.

Ask the children to read the book and give a quick summary of what they think the book is about. Then ask them to look through the book with a partner and discuss how the illustrations make them feel. Ask them to compare the illustrations on pages 2 and 3 with page 21. Why do they think the illustrator has moved from the very dark images to the brightness of light at the end of the story?

Refer to the children's quick summaries about the book from their first reading and then discuss the last sentences of the book "Look! I have wings. Watch me fly!" Ask the children if they think their initial response was enough and if they would like to add anything. To stimulate their ideas, questions or thinking, points could include:

- Does the boy in the story really have wings? Does he believe he has wings? What do the wings represent? Why do you think he says "Watch me fly" instead of just "I can fly"?
- What is Angel House? What does Angel House represent in the story? Can a place affect how you feel?

Discuss how bullying can affect how someone feels about themselves and the bullies. Such emotions might include fear, weakness, frustration, envy and anger. Draw up a list of emotions from the children's suggestions. Ask the children to look at the feelings staircase on pages 22 and 23.

Create a class feelings staircase to explore the issue of bullying and self-esteem, e.g. beginning with "being bullied" and ending "overcoming bullies". Provide the children with sticky notes and ask them to write all the different emotions they think bullying arouses in the victim on the notes. Ask them to place the different notes on the staircase.

Extension work could include an anti-bullying campaign or a creative writing activity on the theme of bullying or other similar issues.

Tigers in Trouble (Geography)

Topic: Animals in danger

Tigers in Trouble explores the theme of conservation and the effect that people can have on the natural world. With simple text and stunning, emotive photography, the book can make a valuable contribution to topics dealing with endangered species, conservation and how wildlife is affected by mankind.

Ask the children to read the text with a partner, this can be done with mixed abilities, and find out three different causes of the reduction in tiger populations.

Make a list of the causes on the board. Ask them to discuss the causes and identify one common denominator.

Encourage the class to discuss the issue and suggest what should be done to alleviate the causes, other than creating tiger reserves. Questions or thinking points could include:

- Tigers are wild animals, so should humans get involved in protecting them?
- What is the reason for poaching?
- Is it more important to save tigers than to provide housing for people? Why or why not?

Widen the discussion to include their thoughts and ideas on other endangered species culminating in a "save a species" campaign.

Extension work could include research on another endangered species, further campaigns and a fundraising event.

When Rosa Parks met Martin Luther King, Junior (Black History Month)

Topic: Discrimination/Human rights

When Rosa Parks met Martin Luther King, Junior explores the issues of discrimination in the historical context of the bus strikes in America in 1955. Extensive use of black and white photography from the period firmly sets the historical context and allows for wider exploration.

Ask the children to read the book and discuss it with a partner. Encourage mixed abilities to get the most out of the whole class. To stimulate their discussions ask them to think about:

- The historical context: How common was racial discrimination in those times? Did most white people think discrimination was fair? Why/why not?
- Personal impressions: How did Rosa Parks feel about having to give up her seat? Why? How would you feel? Are there any occasions when you think it would be right to give up your seat?
- Standing up for your rights: How did Rosa Parks and Martin Luther King, Junior succeed in getting the law changed? Are there any other ways that they could have used? How do people get laws changed today?
- Discrimination today: Do you think people today are discriminated against on race grounds? What is the reason for this? Are there any other types of discrimination? In what ways could you influence people who discriminate against others?

Draw the class together and ask for feedback based on their paired discussions. Encourage the children in groups to draft and write a persuasive text on discrimination. Extension work could include a campaign, research into other areas of discrimination within black history, or creative writing in the form of a diary or letter in role as Rosa Parks.

Top Secret (History)

Topic: Spies in World War Two

Top Secret is a graphic depiction of the activities of Christine Granville, a Polish woman who worked for Britain during World War Two as a secret agent.

Ask the children what they know about spies and secret agents and what role they think they played in World War Two.

Ask the children if they think women would have been good secret agents and give reasons for their opinions.

Ask the children to read the book. Invite the children to give their opinions about Christine Granville. Questions you could ask to stimulate their ideas include:

- Why do you think Christine Granville might have become a secret agent?
- What sort of person do you think would be good at this? What character traits would they need?
- Do you think Christine was brave? Why?
- How would you have behaved in the same situations as Christine?

Draw up two columns on the board with headings: Positive aspects and Negative aspects. Ask children to discuss the story of Christine Granville with their neighbour and decide on three positive aspects of being a female spy and three negative aspects.

Take feedback from the children and add their ideas to the columns on the board.

Ask the children to use the ideas on the board and the text to write a job description and recruitment poster for secret agents during World War Two. This could be done as individual or group work. Extension activities could include researching other influential secret agents and the role they played and creative writing in the form of letters and diary entries in role as Christine Granville.

Using these ideas for inclusion with the whole class in exploring and talking about books can have a beneficial effect on struggling readers' ideas about themselves as readers too. Not only will working with more able readers enhance their interpretation and understanding of texts, but the resulting improvement in self-esteem will boost their desire to read and lead to an enjoyment of reading, helping them make real progress.

6 Collins Big Cat Progress and reading at home

Research has shown that reading at home is an invaluable supplement to the learning that takes place in the classroom.

The parents' approach to reading can have a significant influence on the child's approach to reading and to learning in general. While children read in the classroom and are given opportunities to talk about and question what they are reading, continuing the activity at home on a one-to-one basis allows greater opportunities for them to connect with ideas, emotions and beliefs without infringing on the time or activities of others in the classroom. Reading at home allows children to talk in more depth about books and to practise what they have been learning at school in a relaxed environment.

Parents are generally a child's first teacher from whom he or she learns to use language. Reading at home continues this bond between parent and child. Parents are able to impart their thoughts and feelings while reading and talking about books and they can foster the importance and value of reading.

Parents have a vital part to play as role models, especially as male role models. A child who regularly sees their parents enjoying books is more likely to become a keen reader. And when parents welcome opportunities to read with their child, they impart a positive attitude towards reading which fosters the idea that reading is a worthwhile activity.

Parents are more likely to participate actively in reading with their child if they feel informed and included in what the child is achieving in the classroom. Keeping parents informed through regular updates, newsletters and information about their child's reading progress, what they are reading and why, can help parents feel part of the learning process.

A photocopiable letter has been provided to help parents get the best out of their reading-at-home sessions, as well as individual activity sheets for each book. These provide a way of exploring the themes in the books further, extending learning and reinforcing comprehension.

Dear Parent

Your child has brought the book _____
home to read. Enjoy it together!

How you can help:

*   Read to and with your child whenever you can. When they bring a book home from school, encourage them to read it to you. Find a quiet, comfortable place where you won't be interrupted.
*   Talk to your child about the book, discuss the title and cover illustration. Ask your child what he or she thinks the book will be about.
*   While they are reading, pause occasionally to ask them to explain something, e.g. why a character is doing something, or about a particular piece of information. Talk about the illustrations too. They are an important part of the book and can help your child's understanding.
*   If your child struggles with a word, ask them to sound out the letters to work it out, or to suggest a word that makes sense in the sentence. Don't let them take too long with a difficult word. Prompt them if needed.
*   When your child has finished the book, talk about it together. Ask which was the most interesting or exciting bit. Ask if there was anything he or she didn't understand.
*   Always give lots of praise for their achievement in reading! It will make him or her feel good about the activity and want to do it again!

Be a role model

Children are more likely to become fluent readers when reading is an everyday activity in the home. So share your enjoyment of books with your child and encourage them to join in with the enthusiasm and pleasure that reading gives you.

Follow-on work

Your child's teacher may have sent home an activity sheet to help your child get the most out of reading the book, and extend the experience.

Encourage them to have a go at the activity. Don't be afraid to help or make suggestions, this can reinforce the idea that reading books is worthwhile.

Finally, don't forget to give lots of positive comments and praise. When your child feels they have done well, they will feel good about themselves and want to have the feeling again, making reading a positive experience that they look forward to.

Name

1 The Mission Mars Journey

Draw a story map for Mission Mars.

Write captions to say what happened at each point.

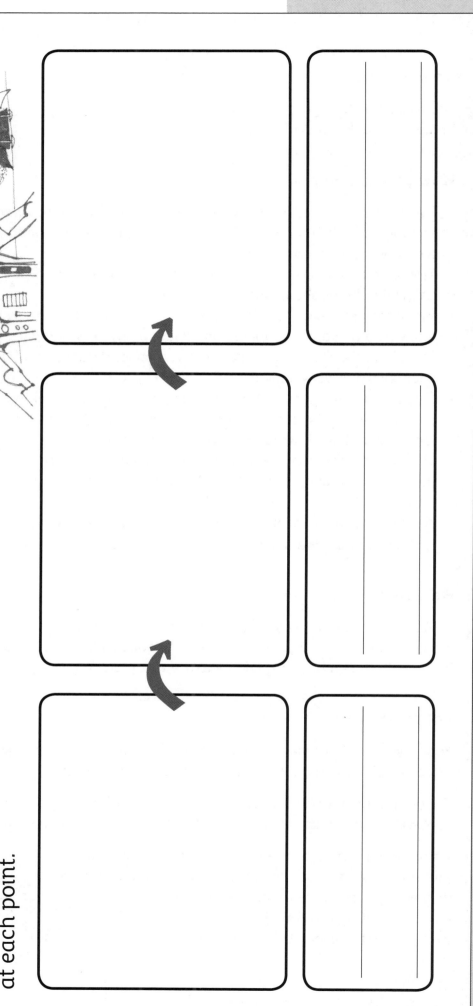

© HarperCollins*Publishers* 2012
This page may be photocopied for use in the classroom or at home

2 Car Cards!

Look at the car cards on pages 14–15.

Create your own car cards for the two "odd cars" on pages 12 and 13.

Cool Cars
Learning objective: Compose and write simple sentences independently to communicate meaning

Name _____

3 Robot Slam

What sort of game do you
think Robot Slam is?

Fill in the table below to tell someone
what the game is about.

Who or what features in the game? Heroes: _____ Villains: _____
What is the aim of the villains? _____
How do the heroes try to stop the villains? _____
How many levels are there? _____
How does a player move up a level? _____
How is the game won? _____

Learning objective: Compose and write simple sentences independently to communicate meaning

4 Olympic BMX Rules

All Olympic sports have rules.

Write some rules that make BMX racing fair for all competitors.

These questions might give you some ideas!

Can you get back on the bike if you fall off?

Can you bump a rider out of the way?

Can you put a foot on the ground?

My Olympic BMX Rules

1 _____

2 _____

3 _____

4 _____

5 _____

Olympic BMX
Learning objective: Compose and write simple sentences independently to communicate meaning

5 Secret Agent Tool Kit

Look at page 4 of the book. It shows the tools used by a secret agent in World War II. What tools would a secret agent use today?

Draw and label a picture of a modern day secret agent's tool kit.

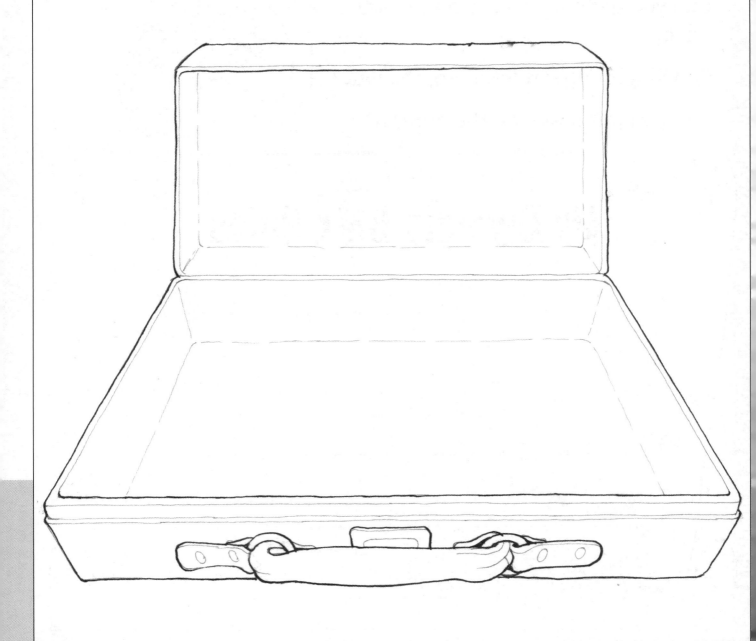

What can you do to keep your muscles healthy?

Design a poster to give advice to other children.

Keeping Muscles Healthy

Muscles
Learning objective: Compose and write simple sentences independently to communicate meaning

Put these statements into the
column you think fits them best.

It's a beautiful and unique
part of the planet.

The world is running out
of oil.

Drilling for oil won't affect
wildlife.

It's melting anyway due to
climate change.

Wildlife would be badly
affected.

Antarctica	
Preserve it	**Drill for oil**

8 Unfair!

Talk to others in your family about what you and they think is unfair in today's times.

Fill in the chart about your ideas.

Things that we think are unfair	What we can do to change it
Some people have nowhere to live.	Ask the government to build more cheap houses.

When Rosa Parks Met Martin Luther King, Junior
Learning objective: Compose and write simple sentences independently to communicate meaning

Name _____

9 Jean's Feelings

Read the words in each box.
They describe how Jean might have
been feeling in the story.

Draw and write what Jean was doing
when he had these feelings.

boastful	**frightened**
_____ _____	_____ _____
ashamed	**relieved**
_____ _____	_____ _____

The Dolphin King
Learning objective: Compose and write simple sentences independently to communicate meaning

Name _____

A Tiger Reserve

What is needed to make a perfect reserve for tigers?

Write five sentences to describe a perfect place for tigers to live. Use the words in the box below to help you.

1. _____

_____

2. _____

_____

3. _____

_____

4. _____

_____

5. _____

_____

| grass | water | space | prey | protection |

Tigers in Trouble

Learning objective: Compose and write simple sentences independently to communicate meaning

© HarperCollins*Publishers* 2012   This page may be photocopied for use in the classroom or at home.

11 **Feeding a Pirate**

Write a menu for having dinner with a pirate. Draw a picture of all the food on the menu.

Menu

Starter

Main course

Dessert

Dinner with a Pirate
Learning objective: Convey information and ideas in simple non-narrative forms

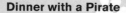

12 My Deadly Creature!

Draw your own deadly creature and write a sentence to describe it.

Things to think about:

Where does it live? In the sea? In trees? In the desert? In rivers?

How does it move?

How big or small is it?

What colour is it?

How does it kill its victims? Bite? Sting? Poison? Crush? Or all of these?

What is it called?

World's Deadliest Creatures
Learning objective: Compose and write simple sentences independently to communicate meaning

13 What's the Story?

Cut out the pictures. Put them in order and
tell the story aloud in your own words.

Seal Skull

Learning objective: Find and use new and interesting words and phrases, including "story language"

© HarperCollins*Publishers* 2012   This page may be photocopied for use in the classroom or at home.

14 Modern Pentathlon

Cut out and put the pictures in order to show how a Modern Pentathlon is organised.

Use the pictures to explain the Modern Pentathlon to a family member.

shooting

running

fencing

swimming

horse riding

Name _____

15 Feelings

Talk about how Sergeant Jackson might have felt at different parts of the story.

Write a sentence to say what was happening under each emotion.

Add another emotion of your own.

bravery

_____

_____

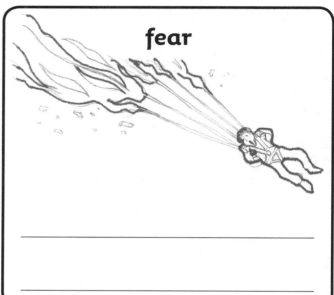

fear

_____

_____

relief

_____

_____

_____

_____

_____

_____

Fire in the Sky
Learning objective: Create short, simple texts which combine words with images

16 ## Who Did What?

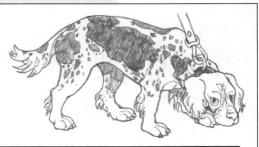

Draw animals in the boxes to show how they helped in war. Name the animals you draw.

carrying heavy loads	sniffing out mines
_____	_____
sending messages	clearing roads
_____	_____

17 Jack and Sam's Feelings

How do Jack and Sam feel during the story?

Put crosses on the emotions graph and join them up to show how their feelings changed.

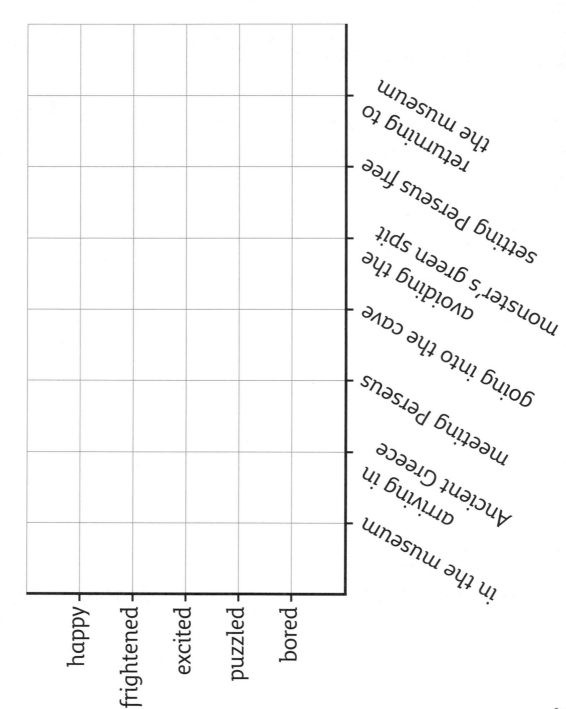

happy

frightened

excited

puzzled

bored

in the museum

arriving in Ancient Greece

meeting Perseus

going into the cave

avoiding the monster's green spit

setting Perseus free

returning to the museum

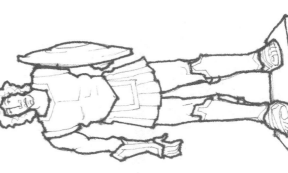

The Deadly Monster
Learning objective: Convey information and ideas in simple non-narrative forms

Name _____

18 Natural Disasters

Read the chart about natural disasters on pages 22–23. Add key words on each disaster to the chart.

Disaster	Cause	Effect	What to do?
Hurricane	High winds	Blows down buildings	Move to a safe place.
Volcano			
Earthquake			
Tsunami			

Learning objective: Compose and write simple sentences independently to communicate meaning

Name _____

19 Text-a-Spell

Can you work out what these text wishes say?

Write out the wish in full and what might go wrong with each one.

1. I wish 4 a Fairy Gmother

_____

_____

2. Snd a prty drss 2 me

_____

_____

3. Snd ADR pls

_____

_____

4. I wd like a prpl prty drss

_____

_____

Zara and the Fairy Godbrother
Learning objective: Segment sounds in order to spell longer words
© HarperCollins*Publishers* 2012   This page may be photocopied for use in the classroom or at home.

Name _____

Food Miles

Look in your fridge and food cupboards.
Check the labels of your food to find out
where it has come from.

Write the countries next to the food.
Add any more of your own that aren't listed.

Type of food	Where it's from
cheese	
eggs	
orange juice	
tea	
sugar	
rice	
baked beans	

Learning objective: Segment sounds in order to spell longer words
© HarperCollins*Publishers* 2012   This page may be photocopied for use in the classroom or at home.

Name _____

21 My Special Place

Do you ever want to be somewhere on your own, to escape from noisy brothers or sisters or parents?

What would your special place be like? Draw a picture of it and write a short description.

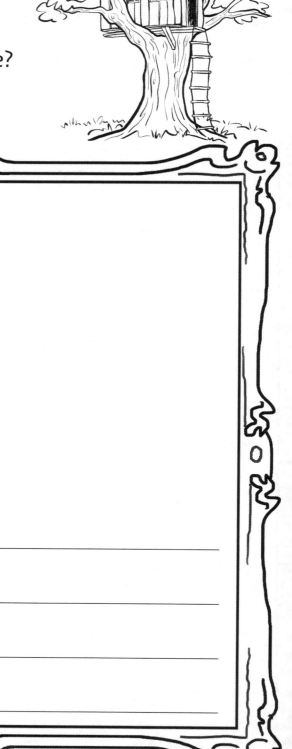

Angel House

Learning objectives: Create short, simple texts which combine words with images

© HarperCollins*Publishers* 2012   This page may be photocopied for use in the classroom or at home.

Look at these headlines and at the photos on pages 22–23.

Lost in the desert
Swimmer bites back
Life-saving landing
A remarkable rescue
Three boys lost at sea

Write short newspaper headlines for the other amazing escapes in the book.

Re-read the information and try to make your headlines eye-catching.

Amazing escape	Newspaper headline
A plane crashed in the Indian Ocean. Only one girl survived.	
A shark swallowed a diver's head in Australia.	
A skier was trapped in an avalanche.	

Learning objective: Convey information and ideas in simple non-narrative forms
© HarperCollins*Publishers* 2012   This page may be photocopied for use in the classroom or at home.

Name

23 Winkie's Journey

Mark crosses on the graph and then join them up to show how exciting Winkie's journey was.

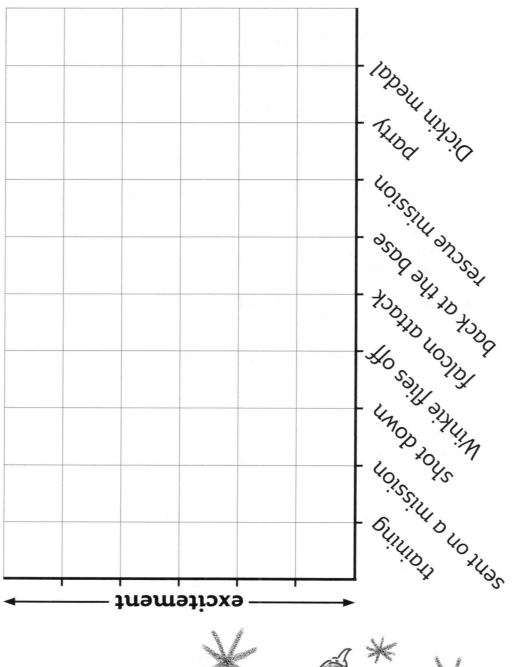

excitement

training

sent on a mission

shot down

Winkie flies off

falcon attack

back at the base

rescue mission

party

Dickin medal

Winkie's War

Name _____

Good and Bad Times

How would you feel about the different aspects of growing up in wartime?

Write a positive and a negative sentence for each activity. One has been done for you.

	Positive	Negative
Wearing a gas mask	It might save your life.	It feels uncomfortable.
Going to school		
Going to the countryside		
Being sent away from your family		
Free milk and fruit juice		
Toys made of cardboard		
Sleeping in the London underground		

Growing up in Wartime

Learning objective: Compose and write simple sentences independently to communicate meaning

© HarperCollins*Publishers* 2012   This page may be photocopied for use in the classroom or at home.

Notes